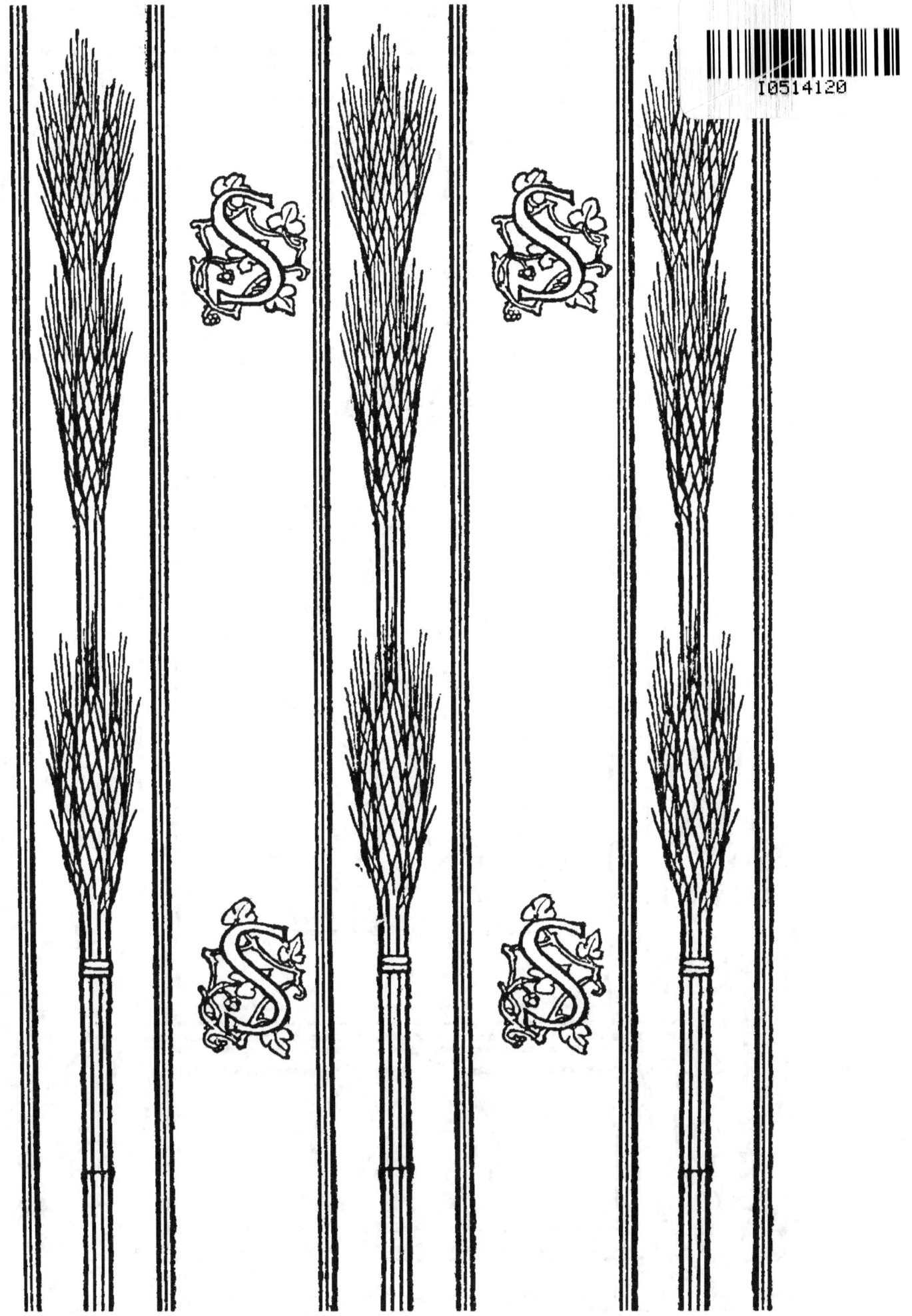

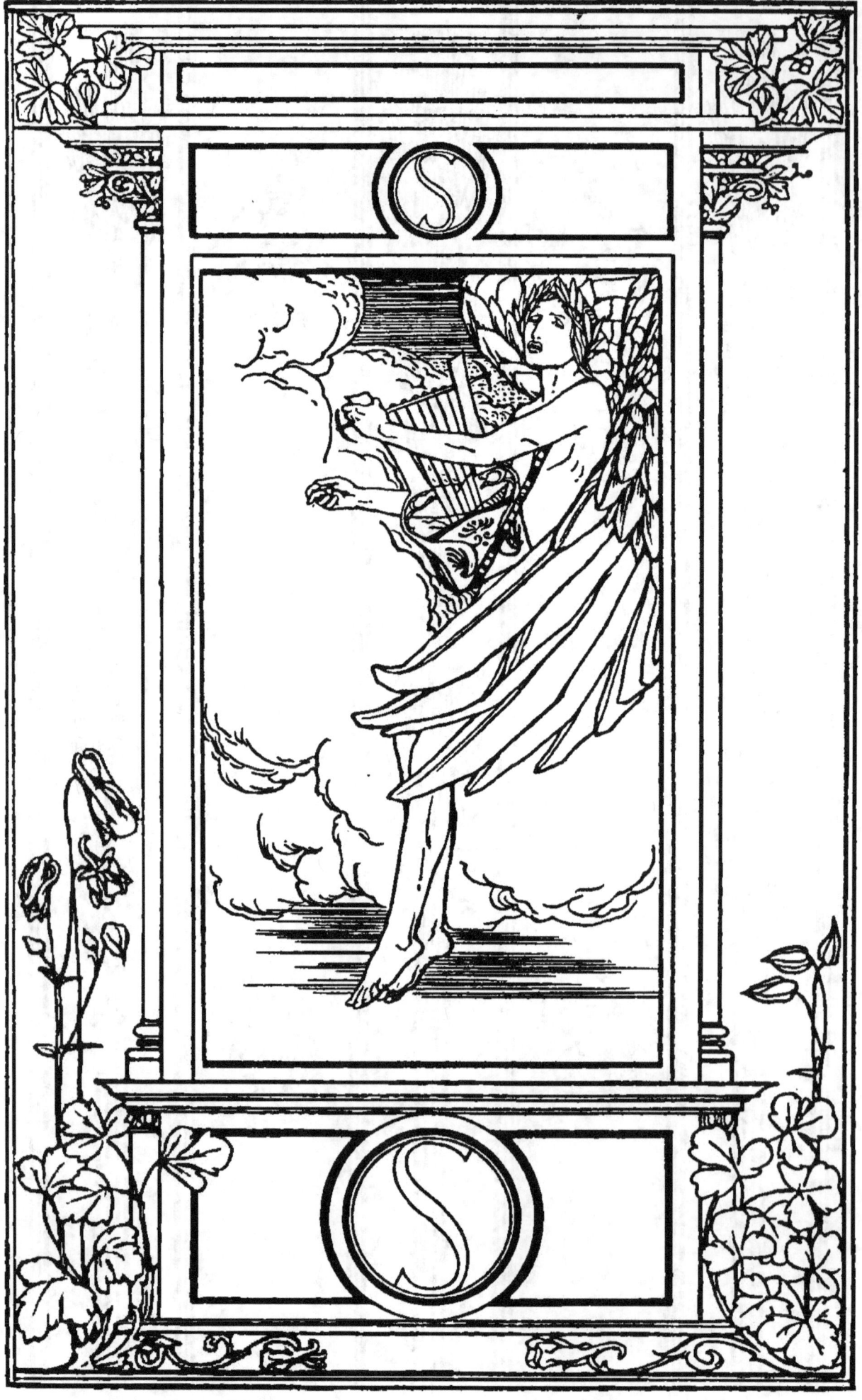

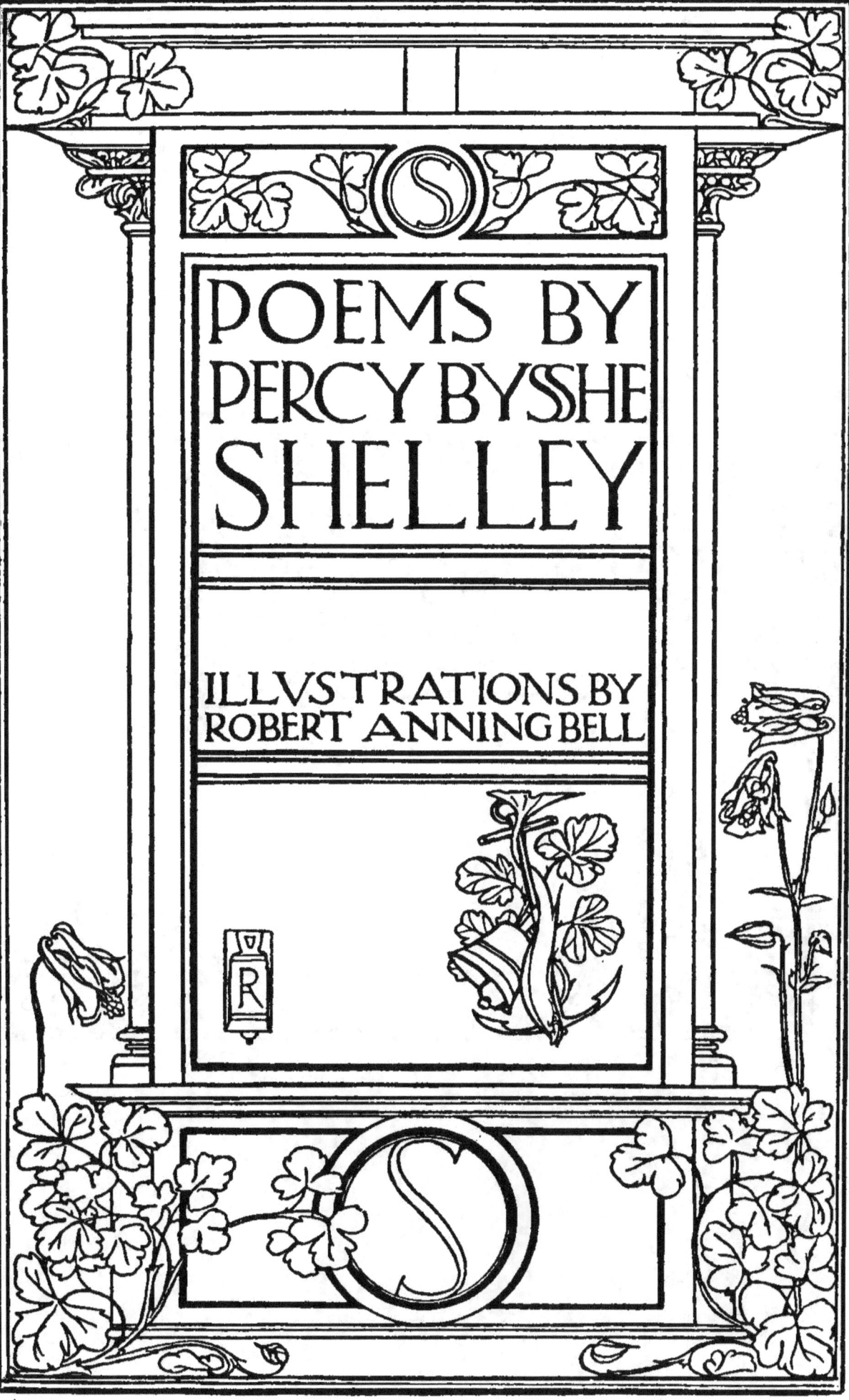

POEMS BY PERCY BYSSHE SHELLEY

ILLVSTRATIONS BY ROBERT ANNING BELL

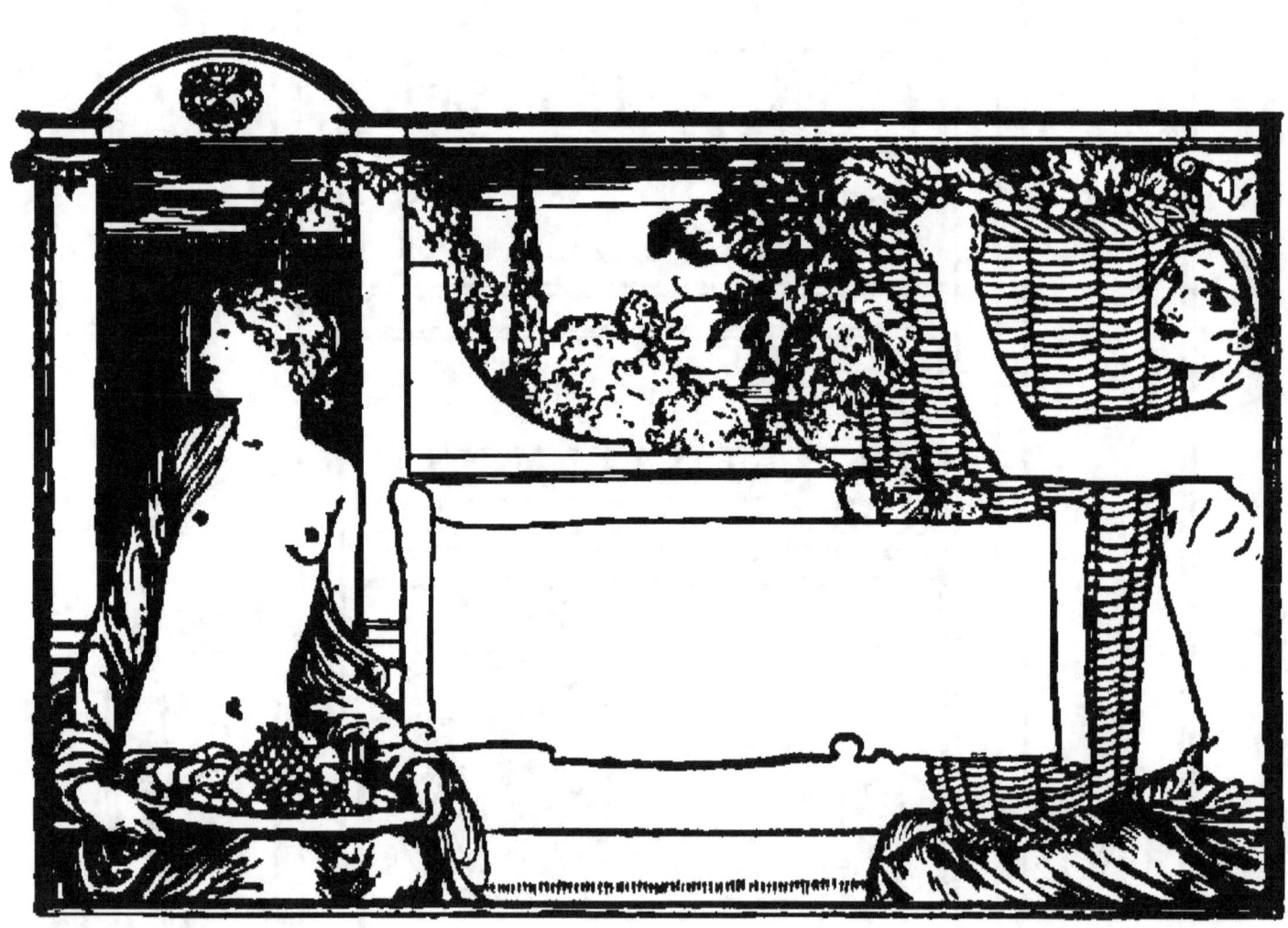

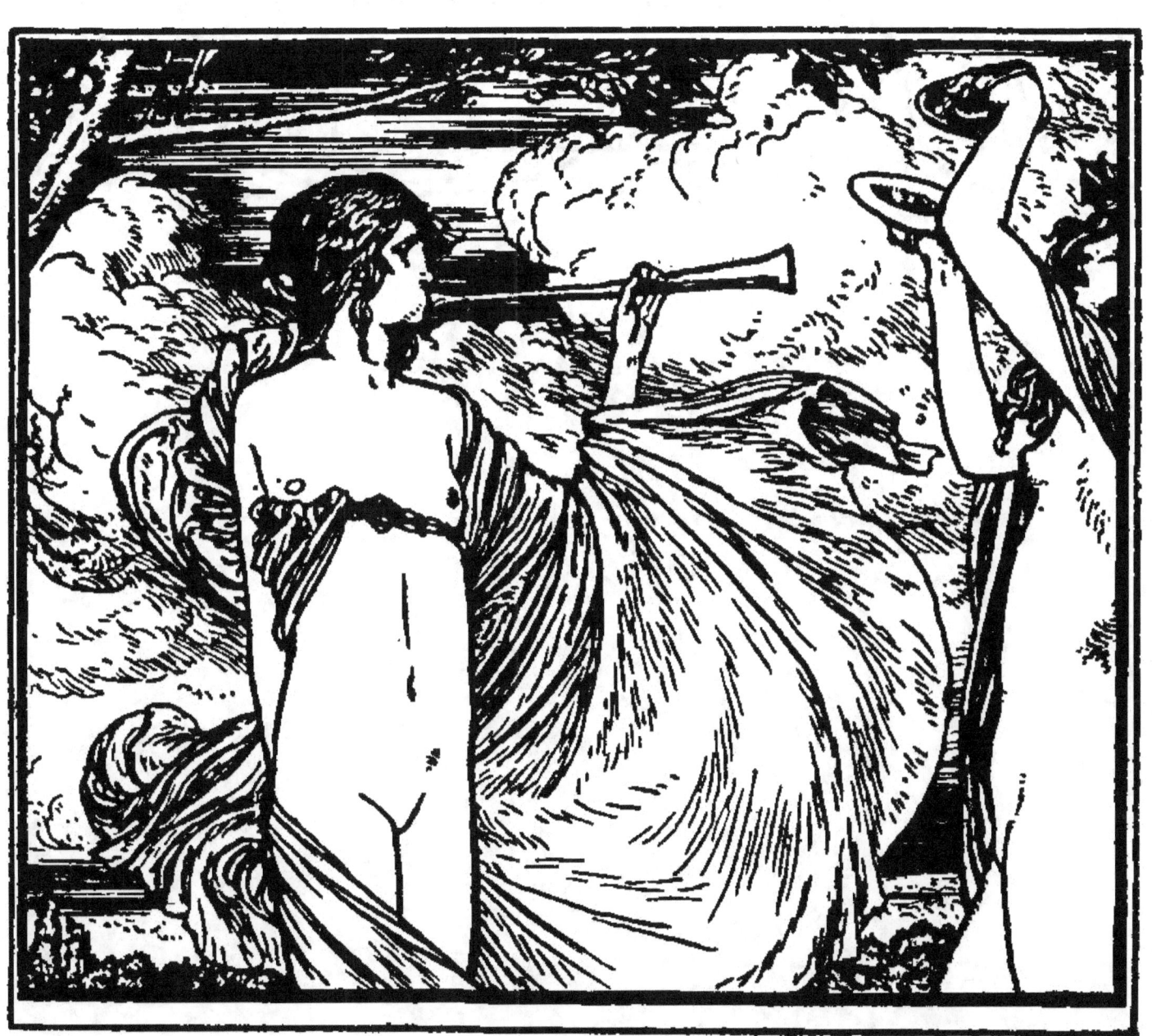

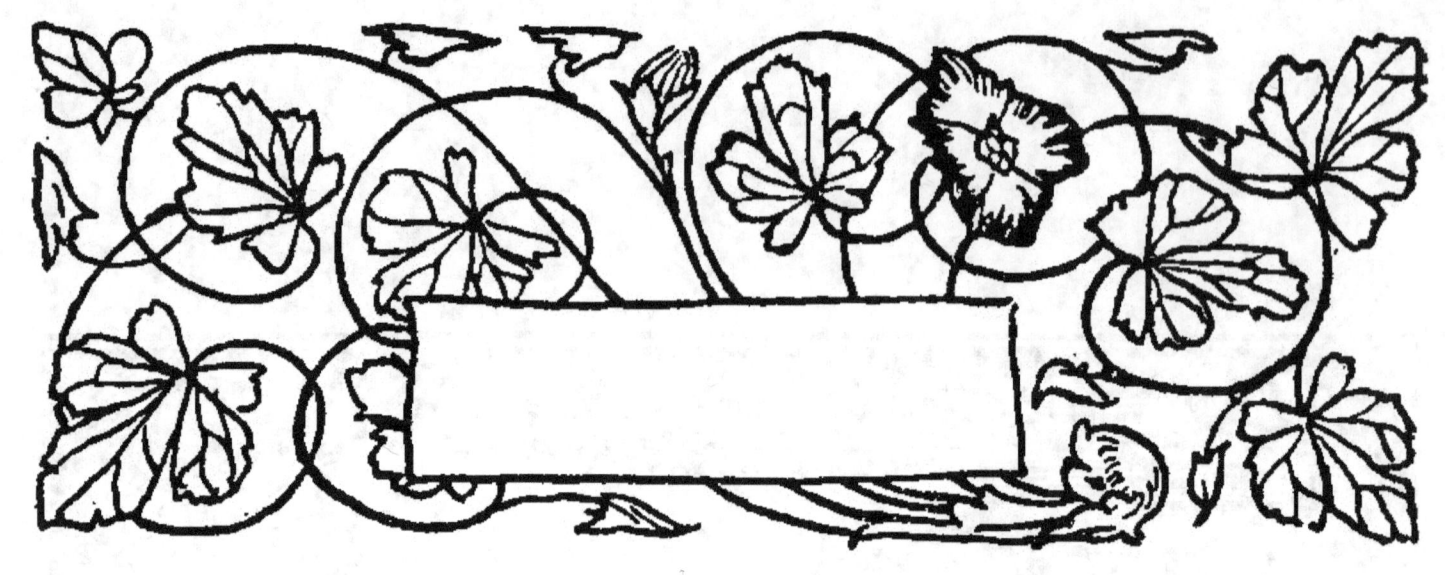

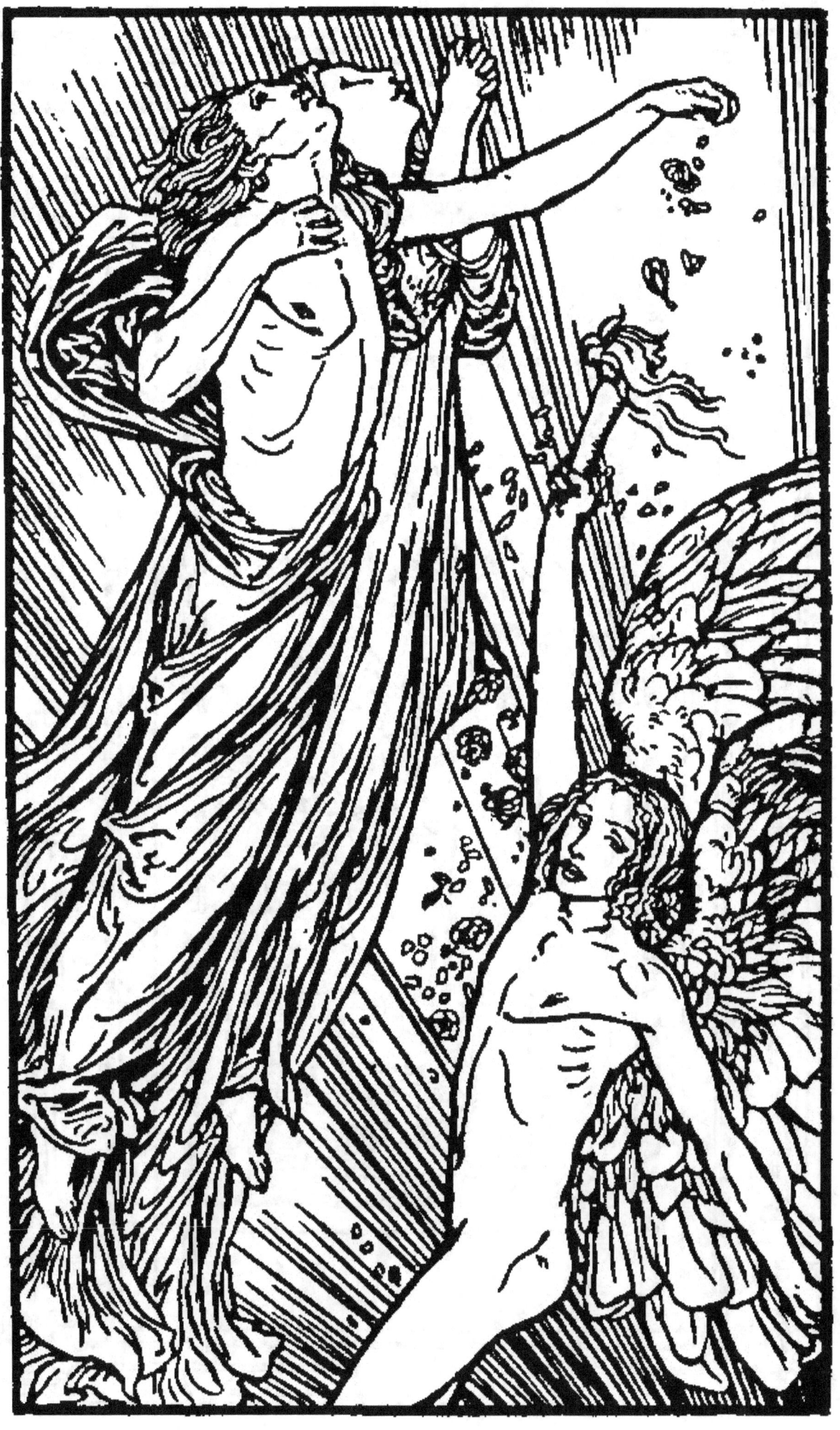

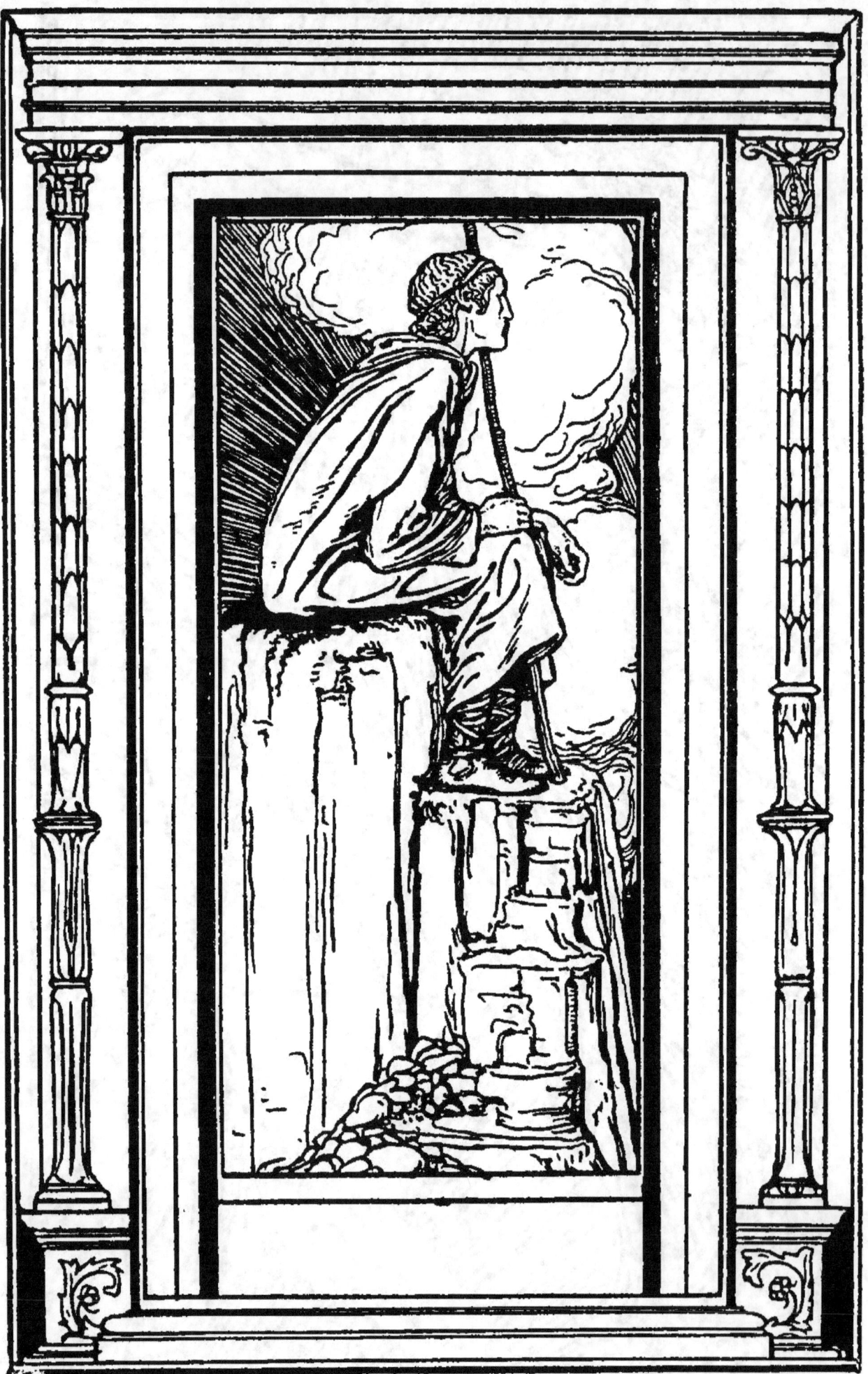

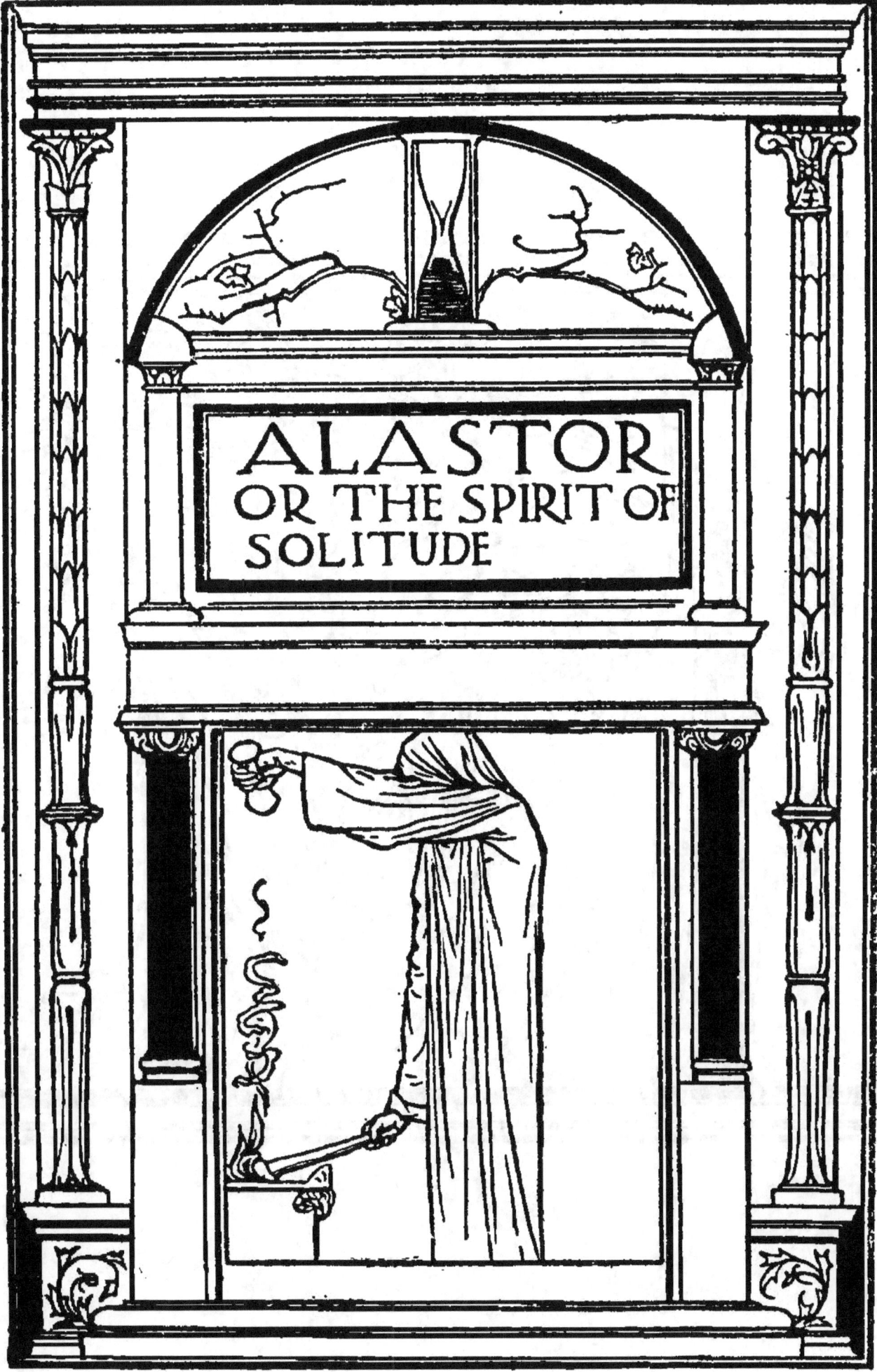

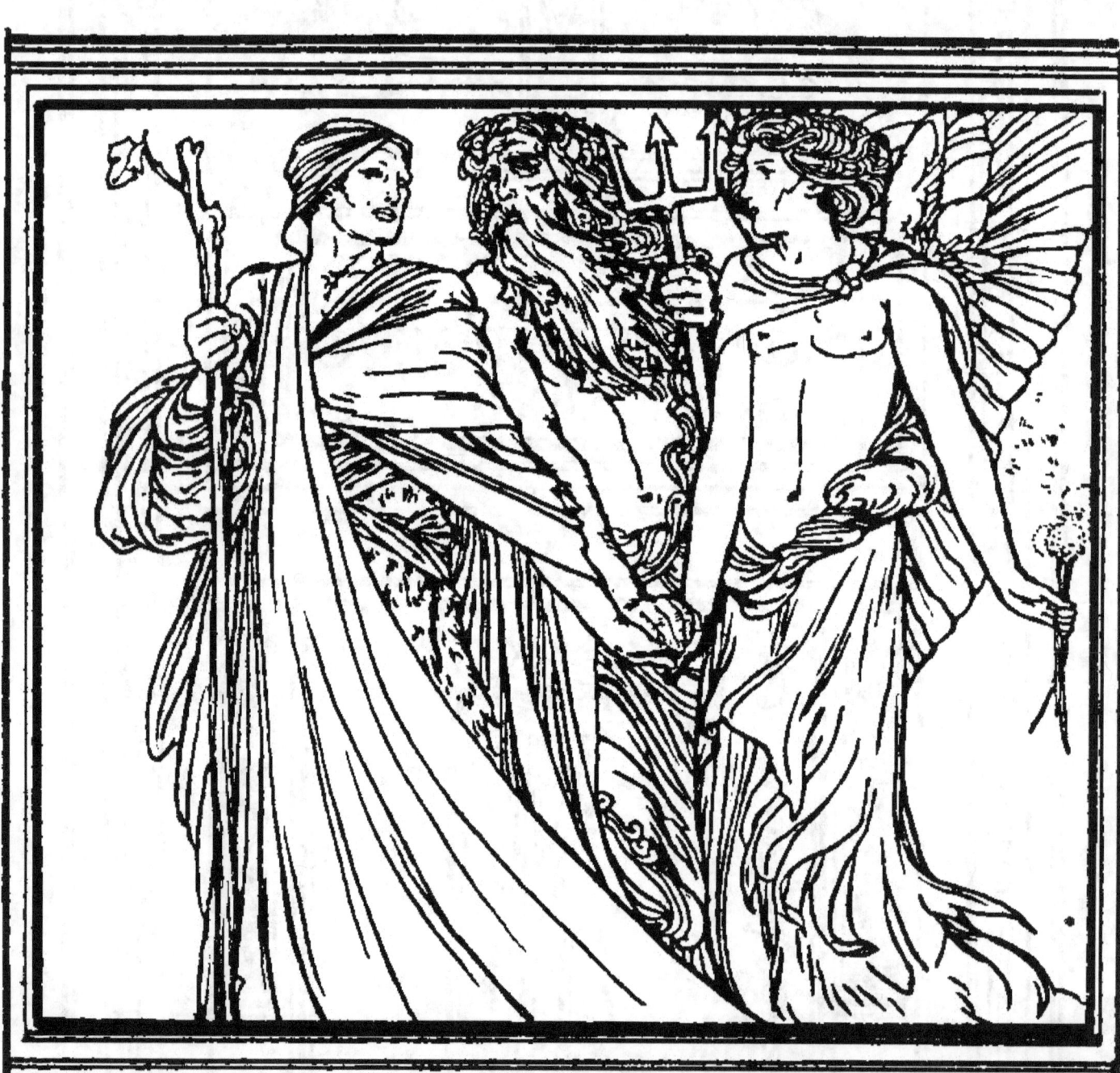

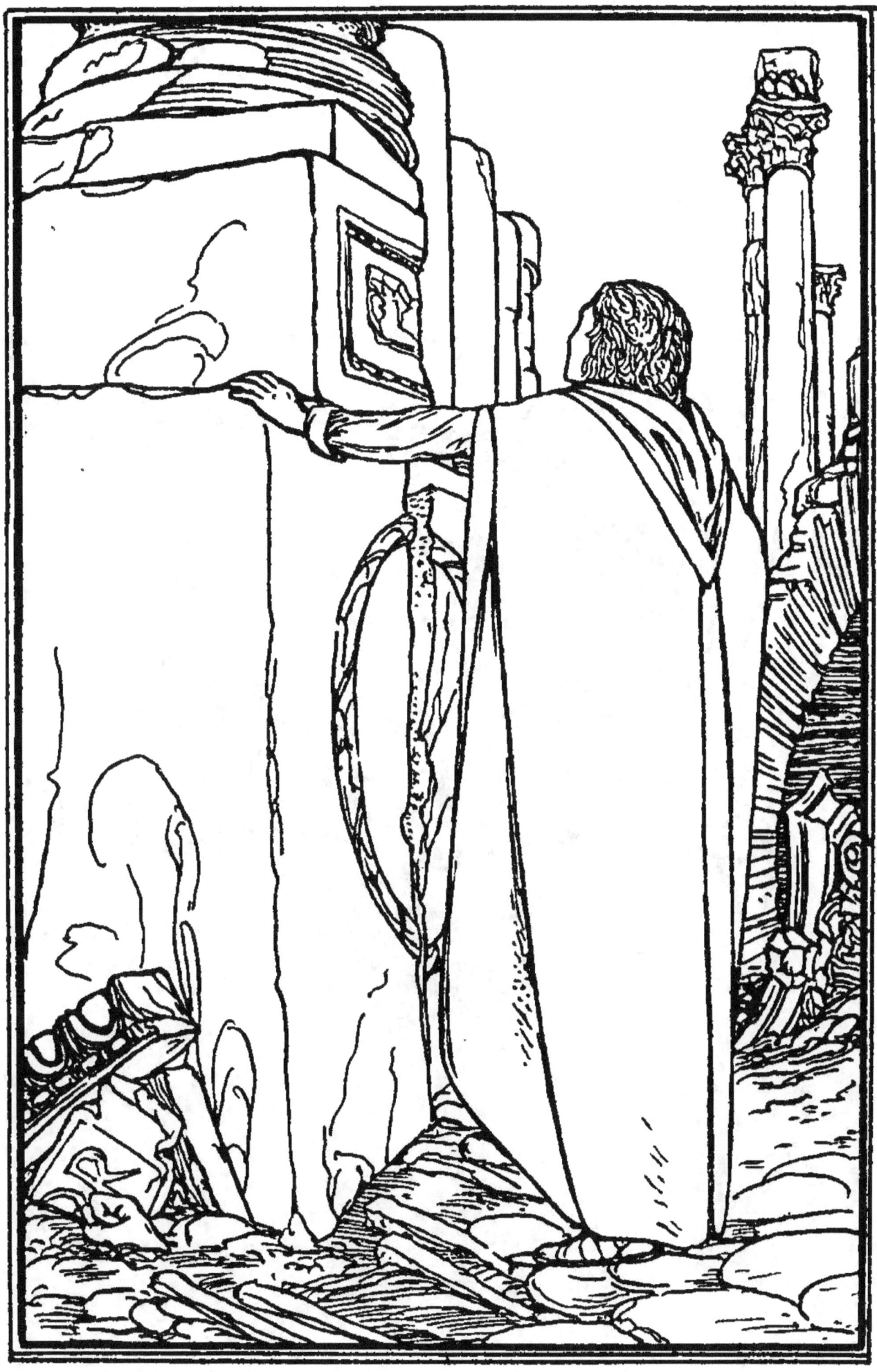

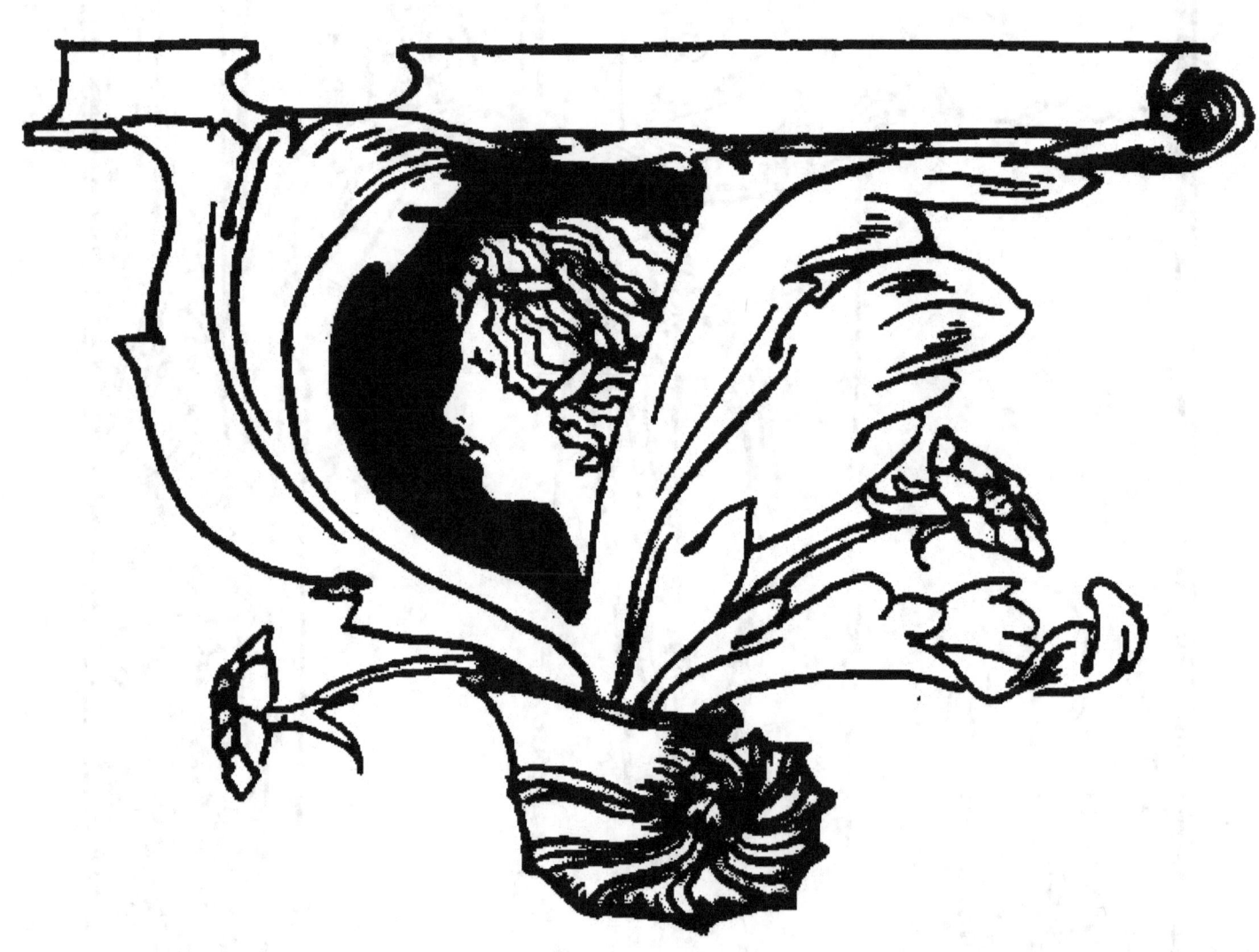

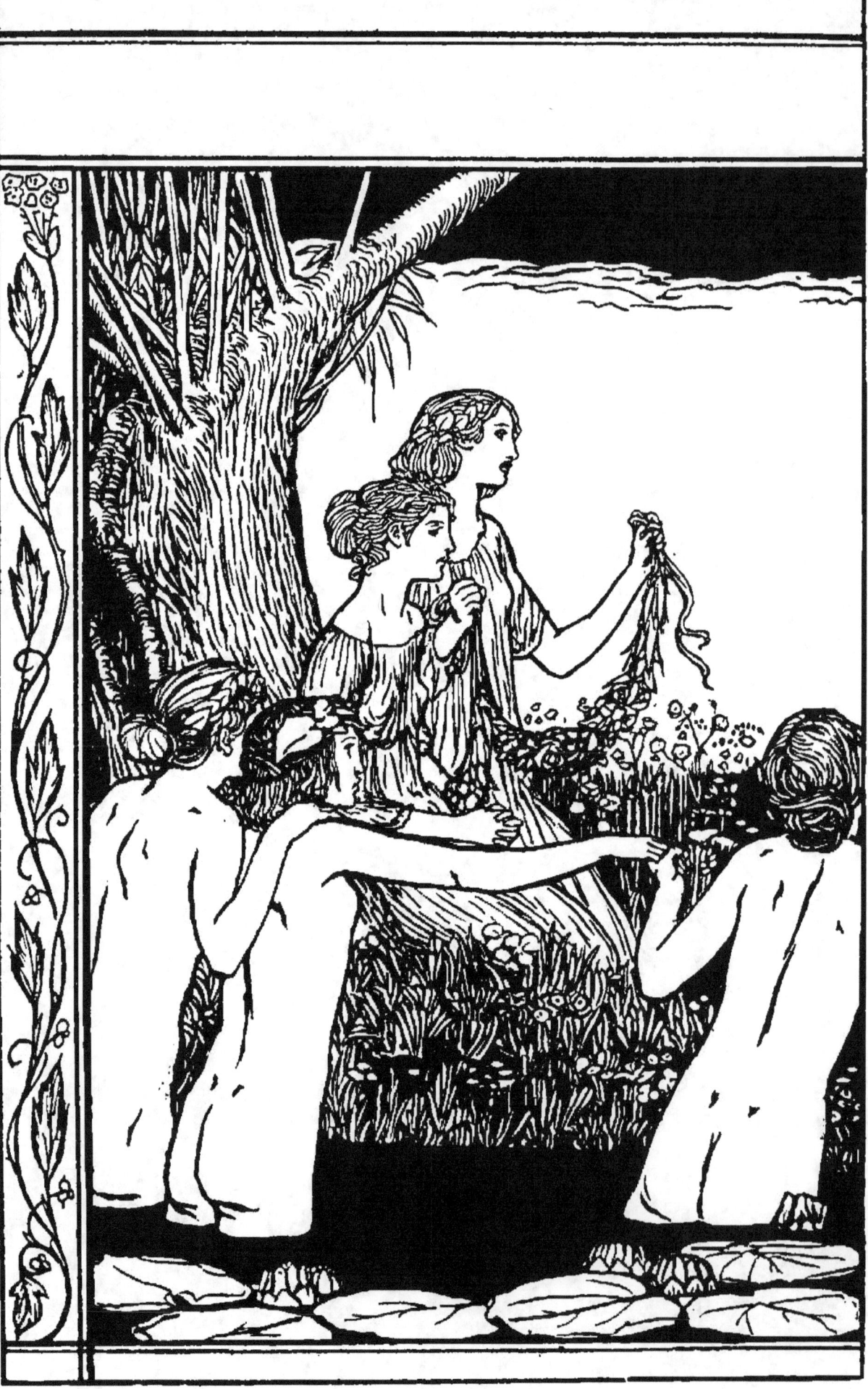

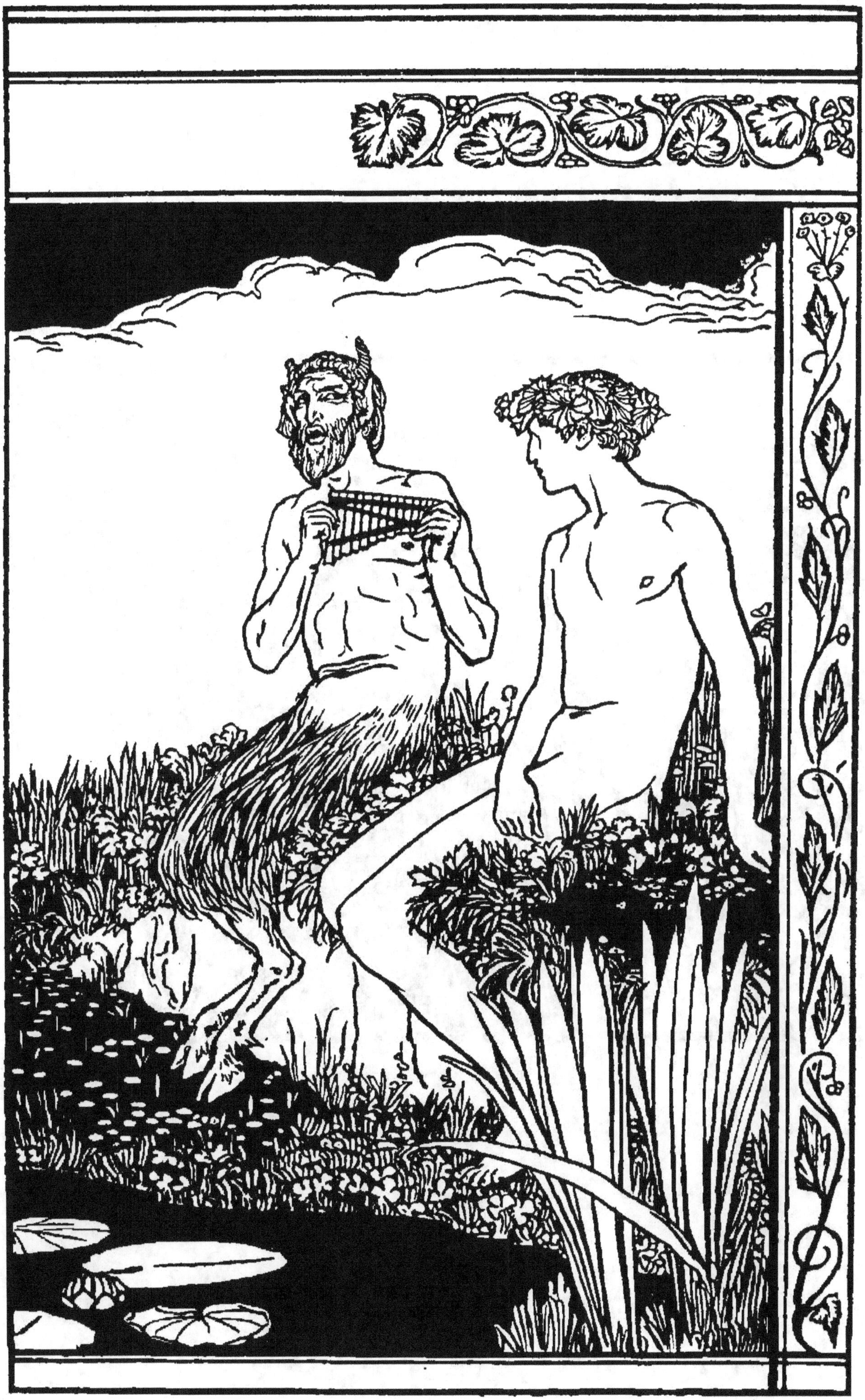

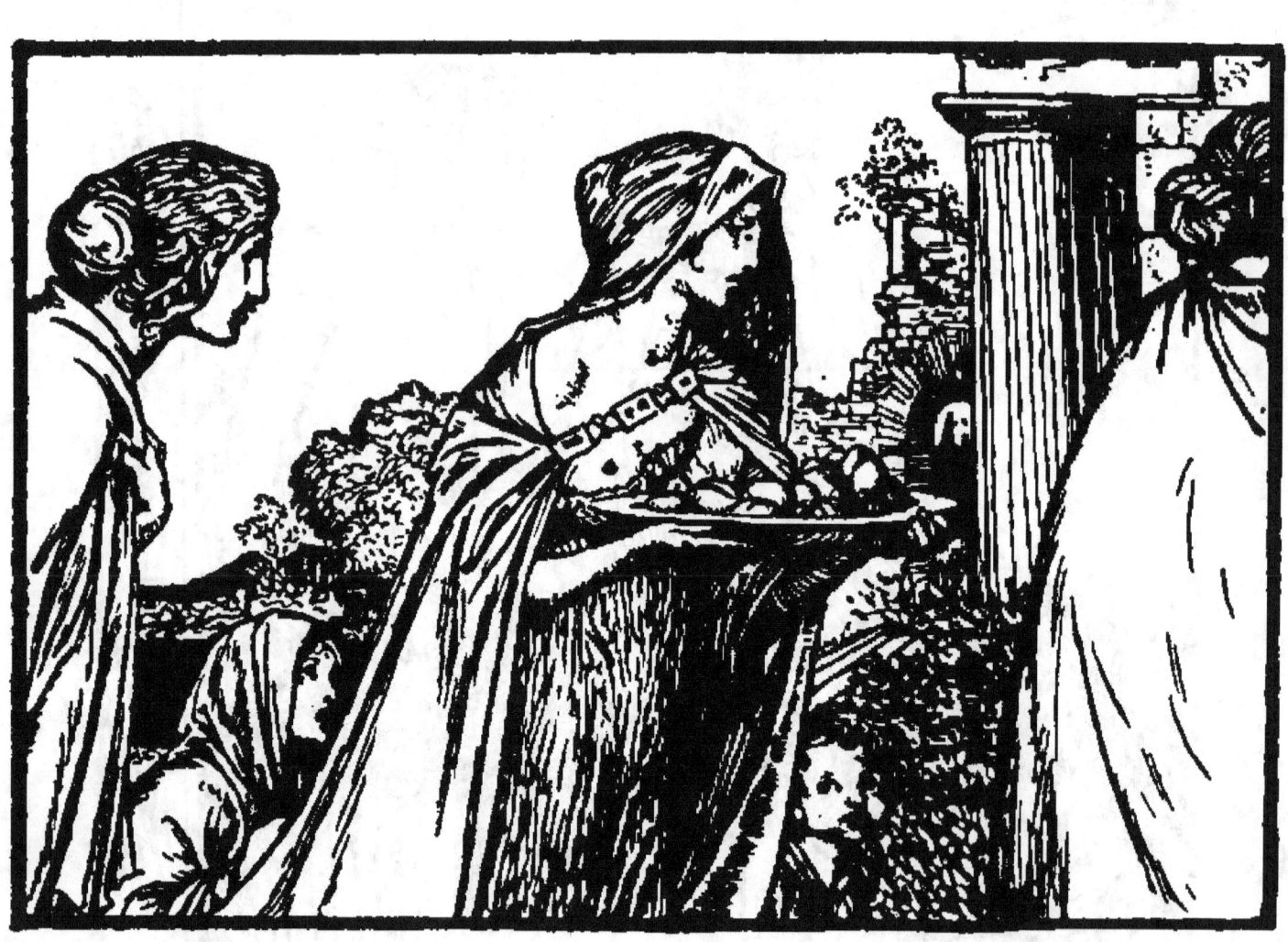

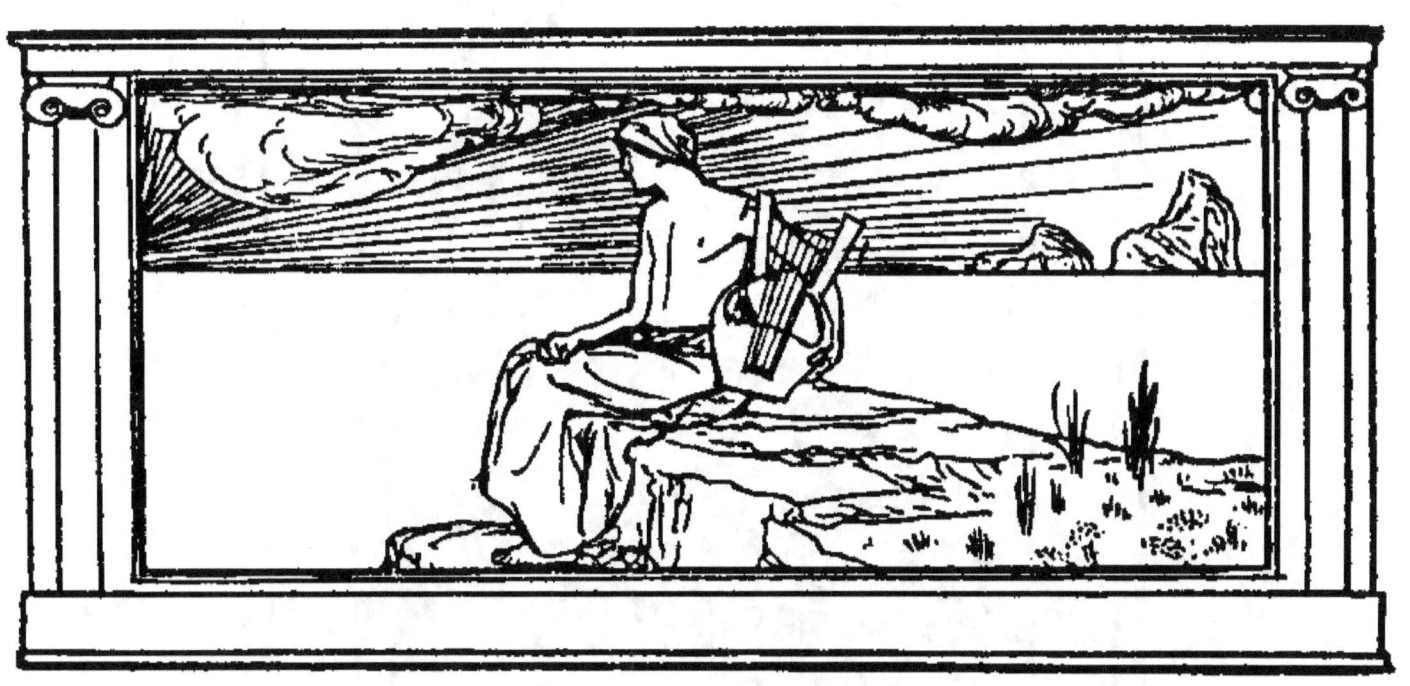

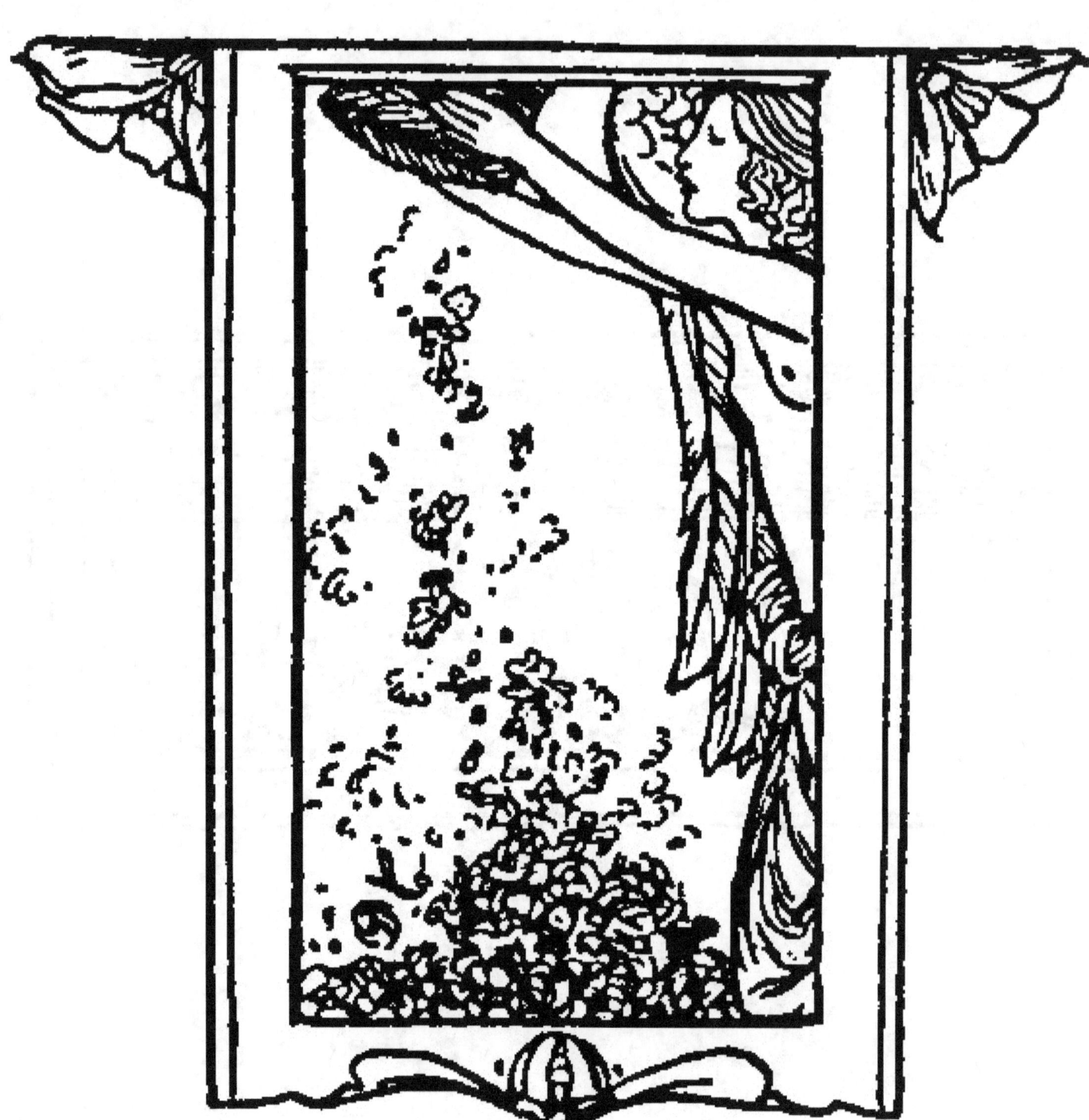

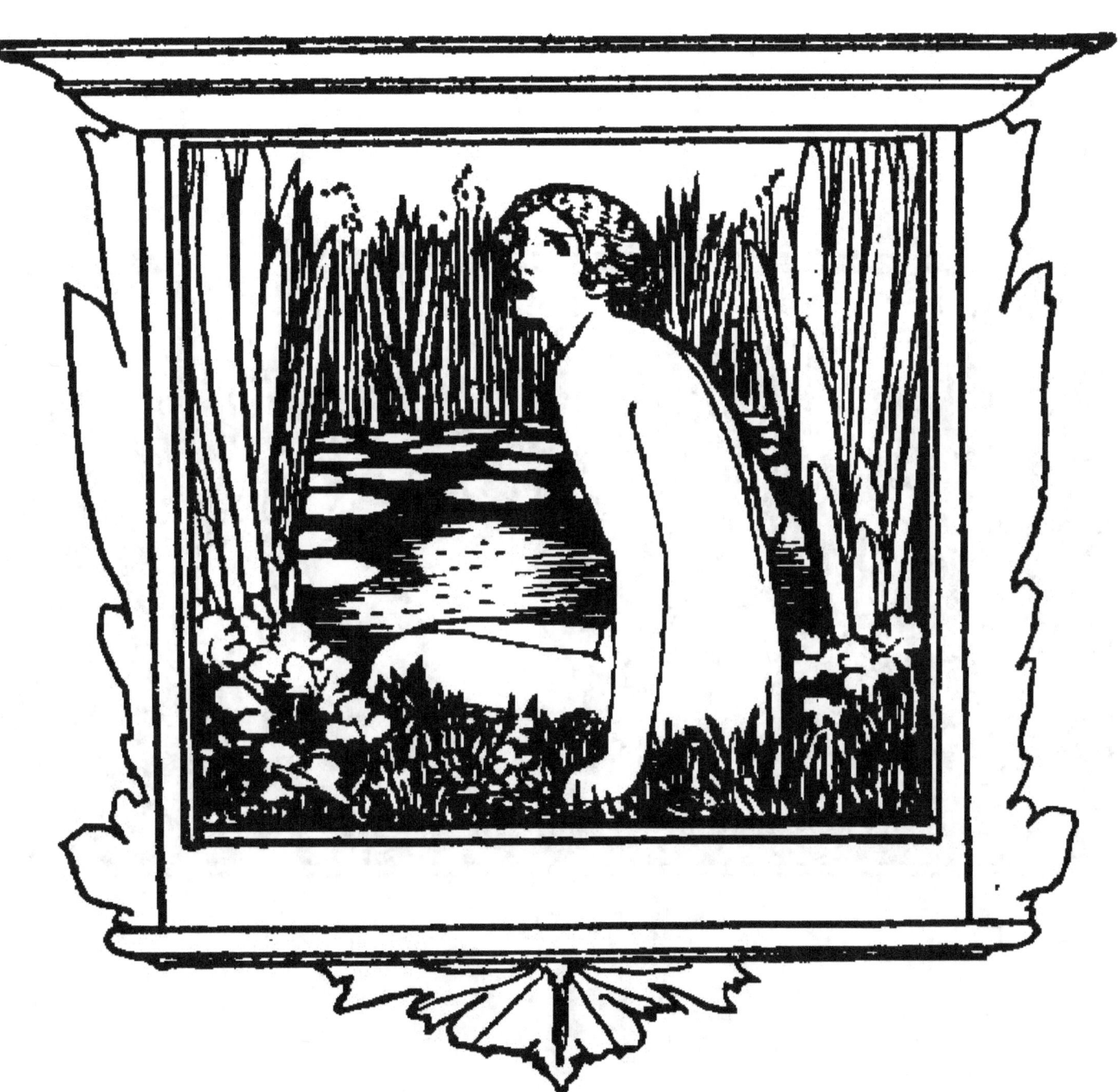

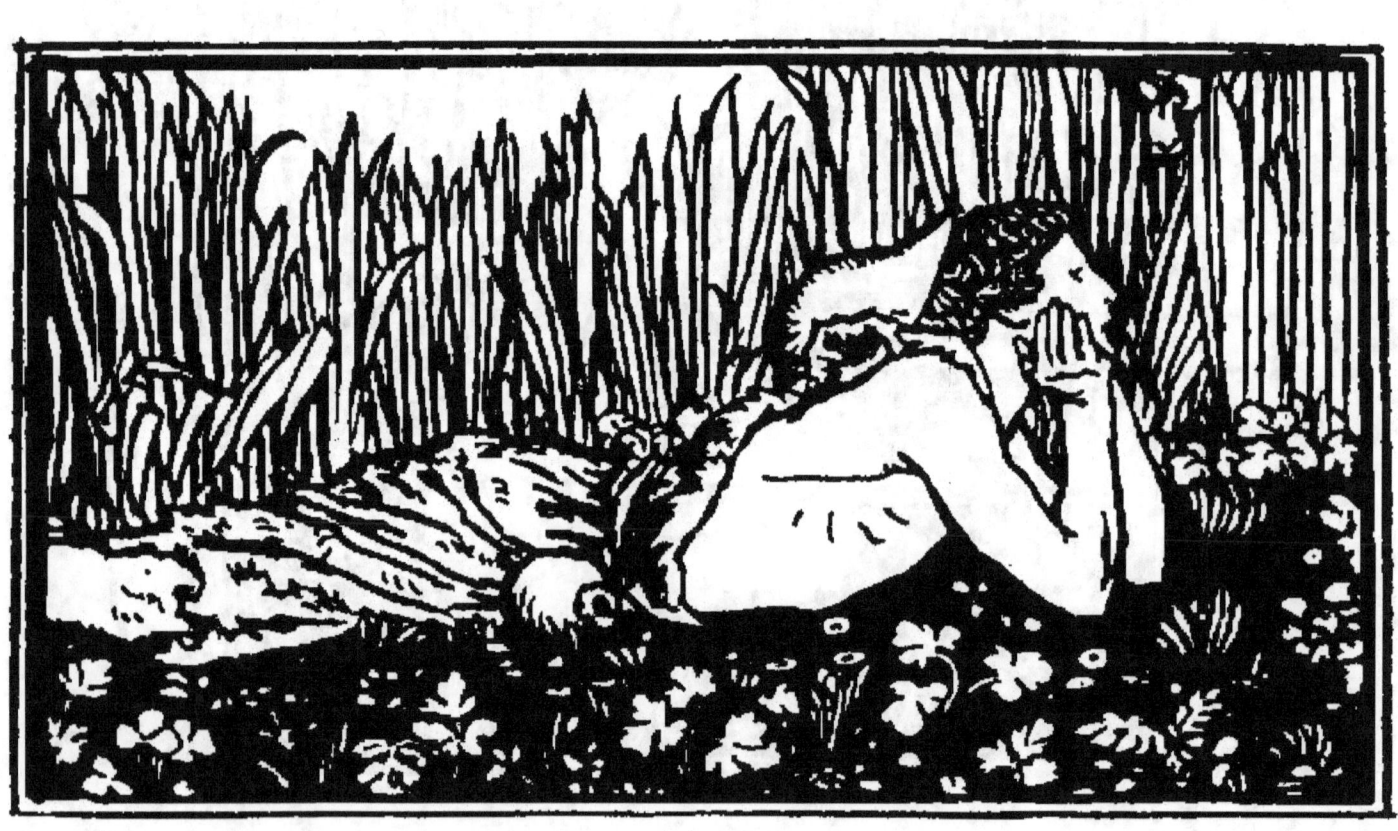

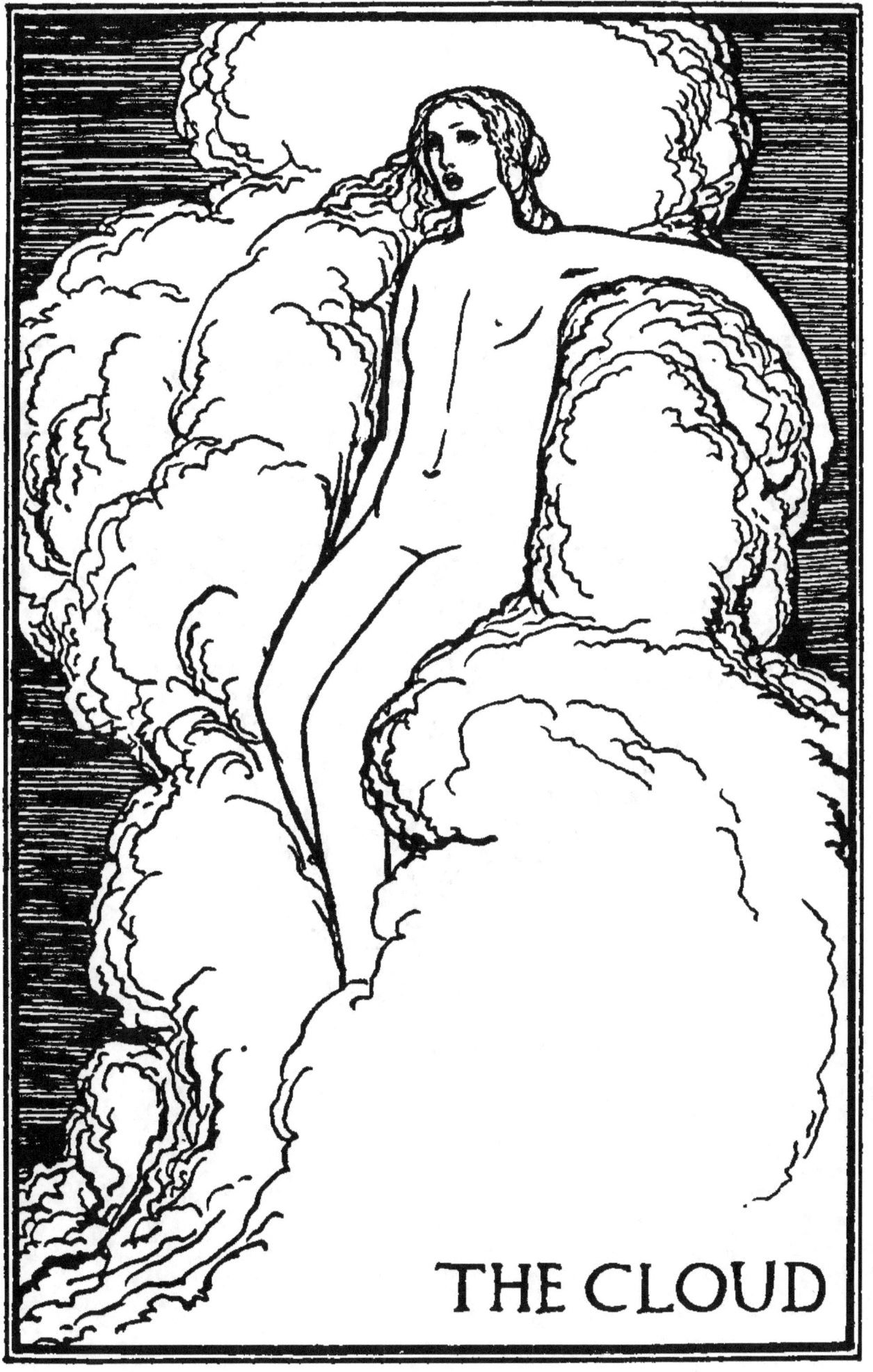

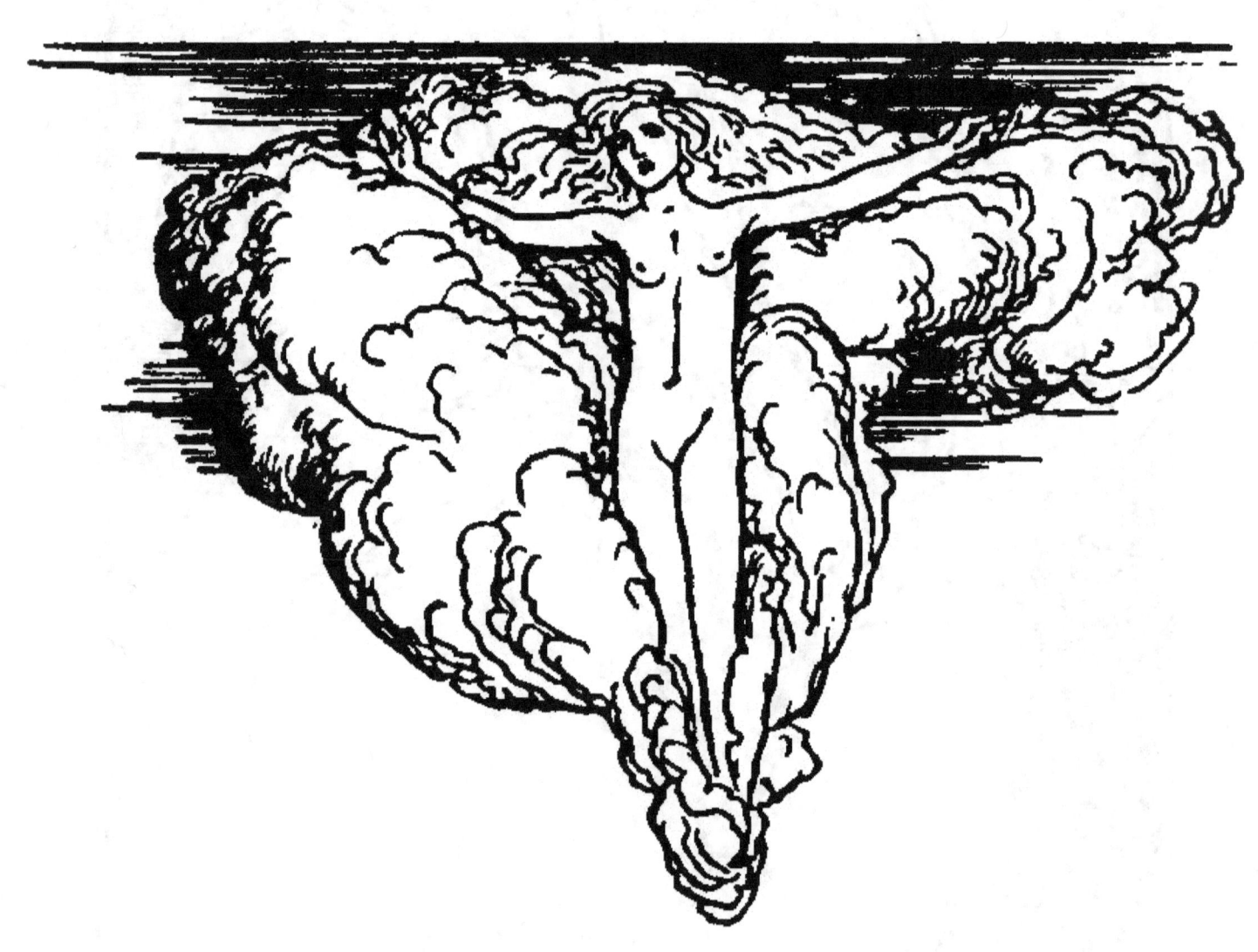

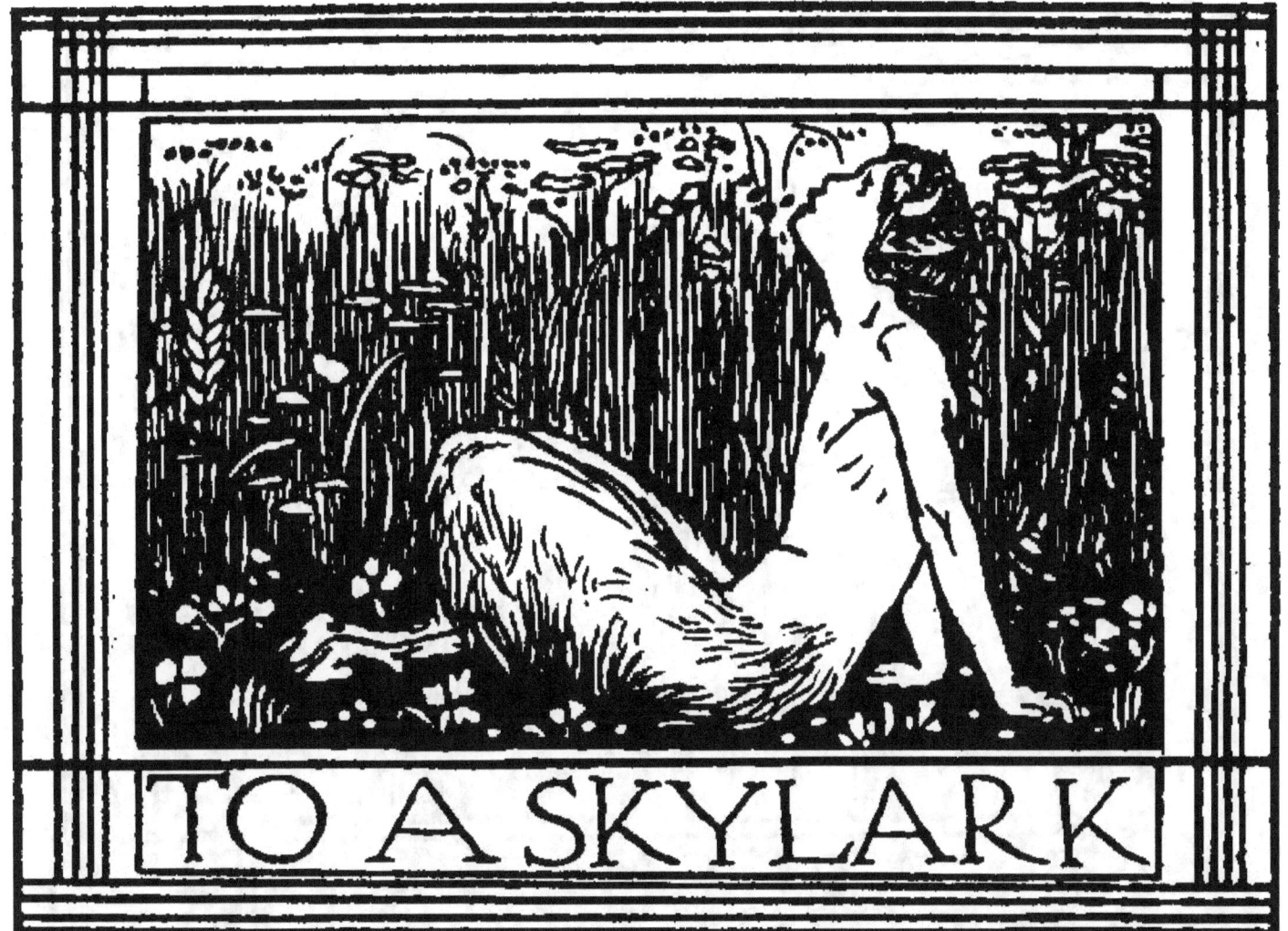

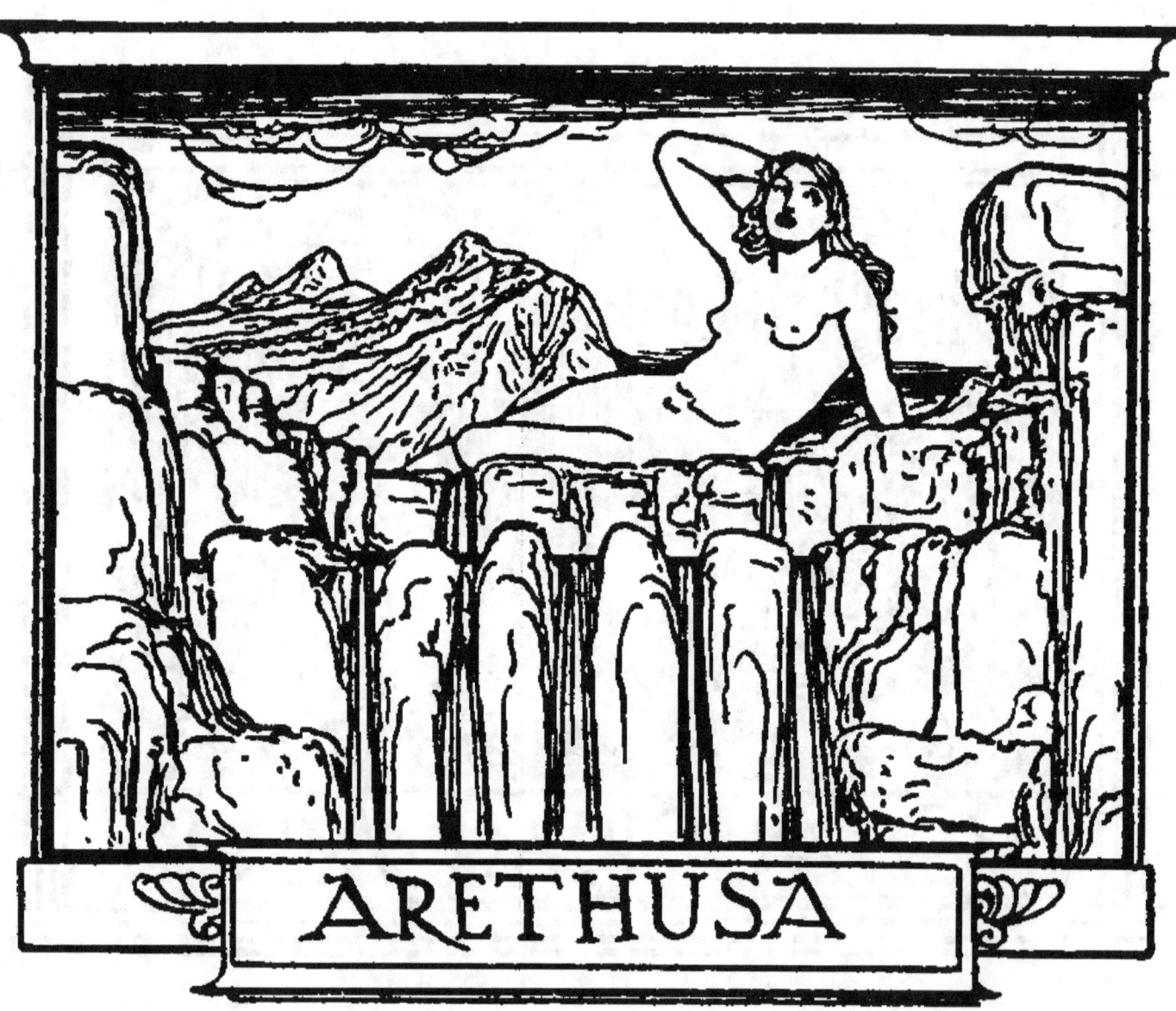

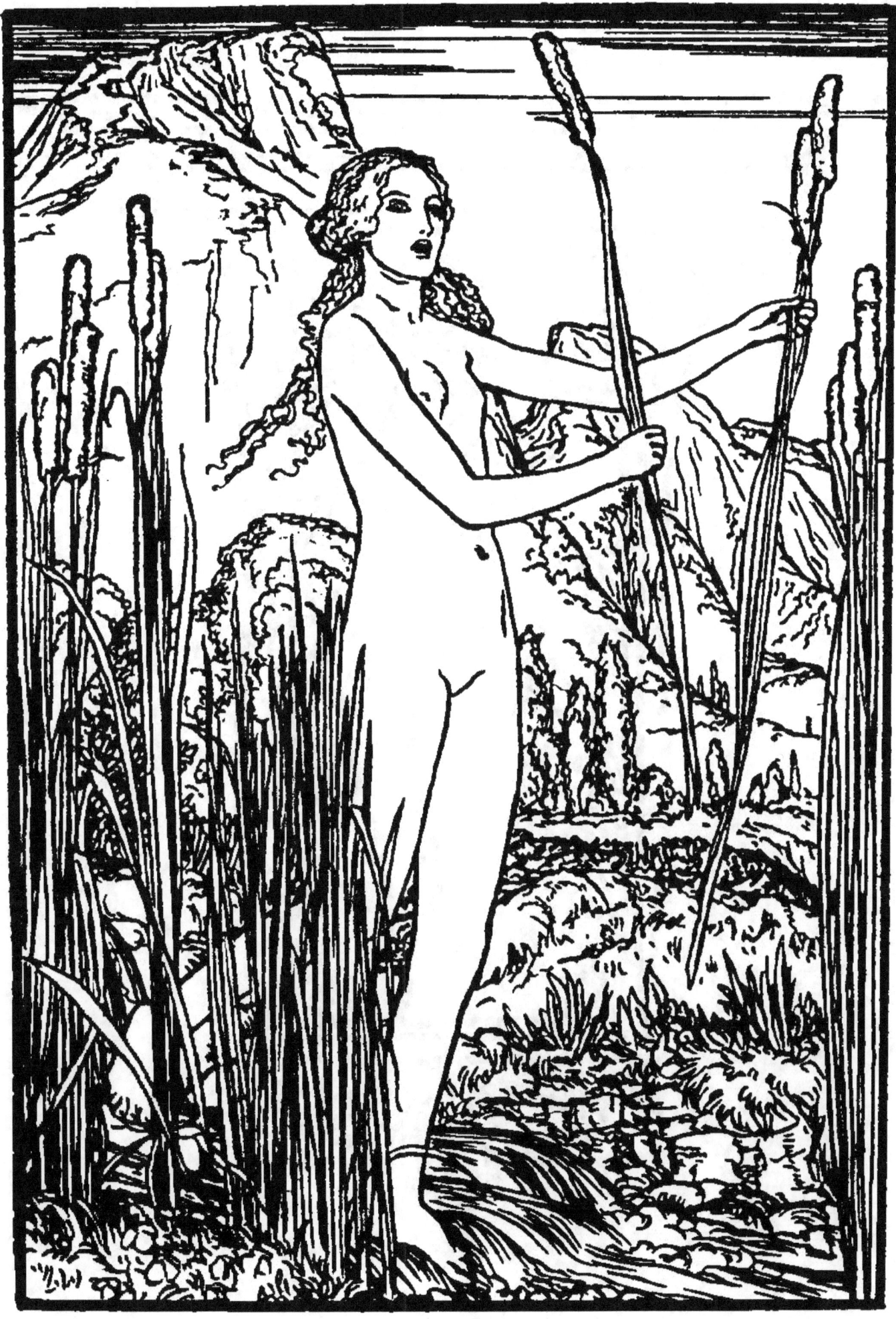

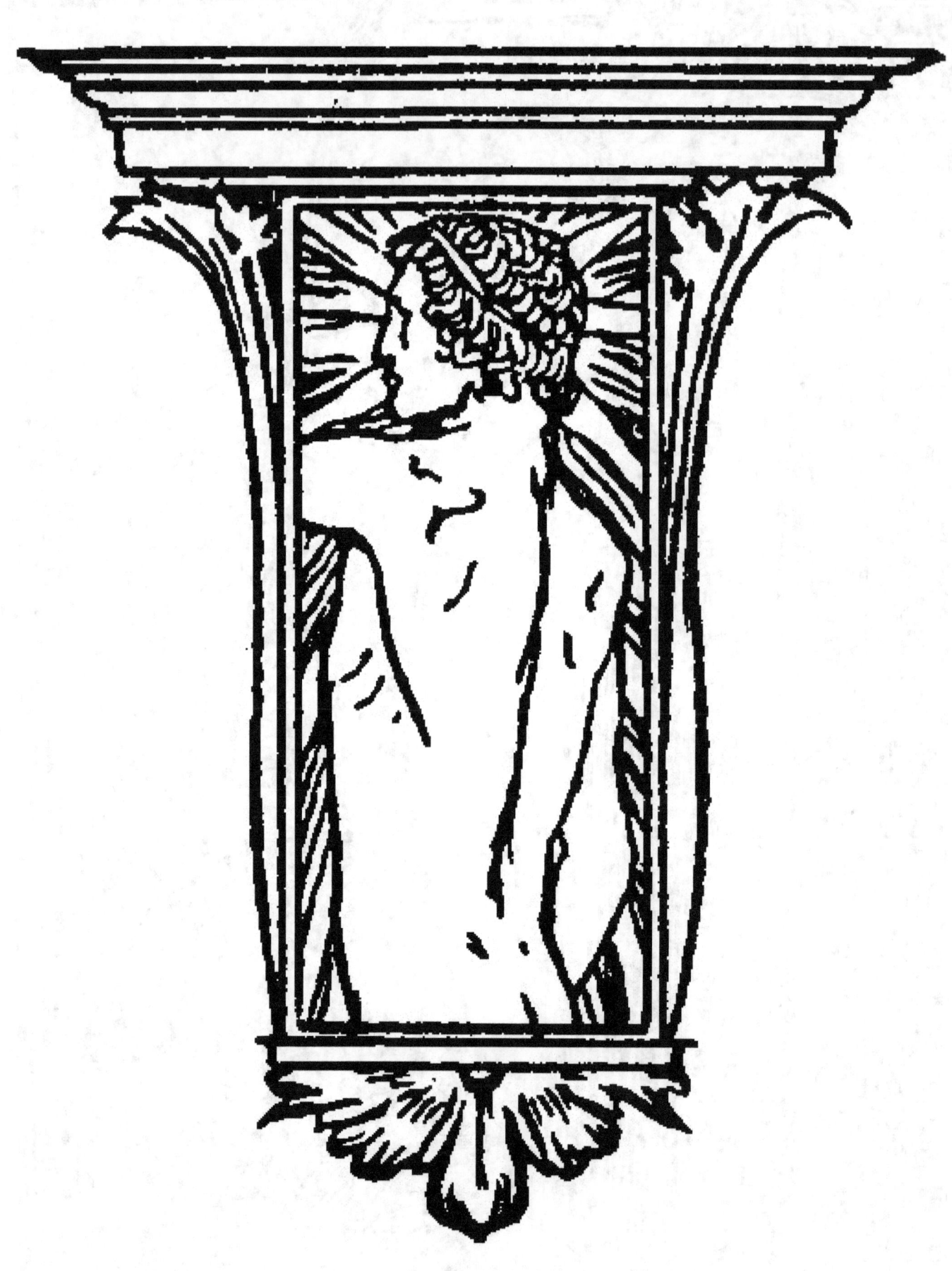

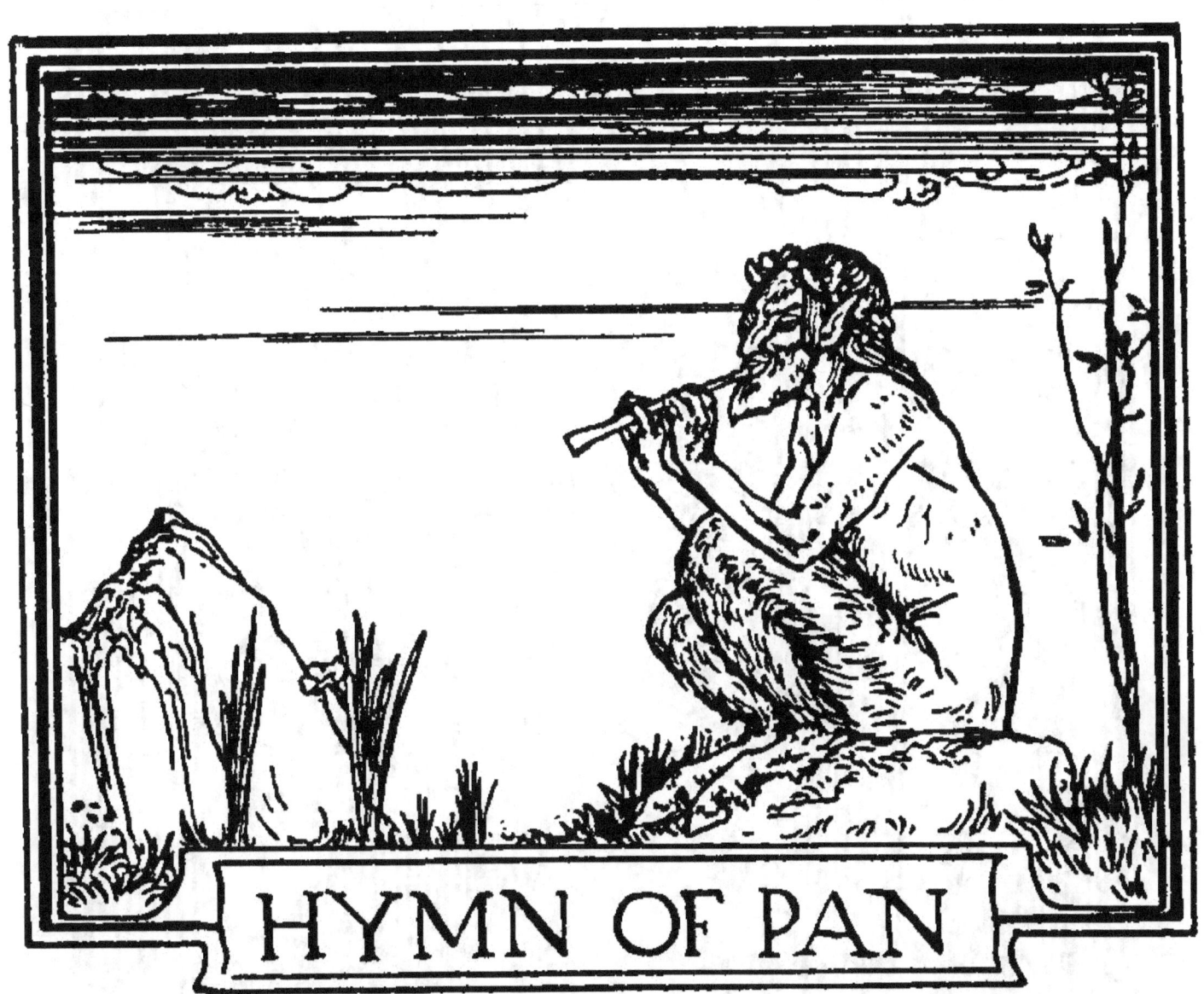

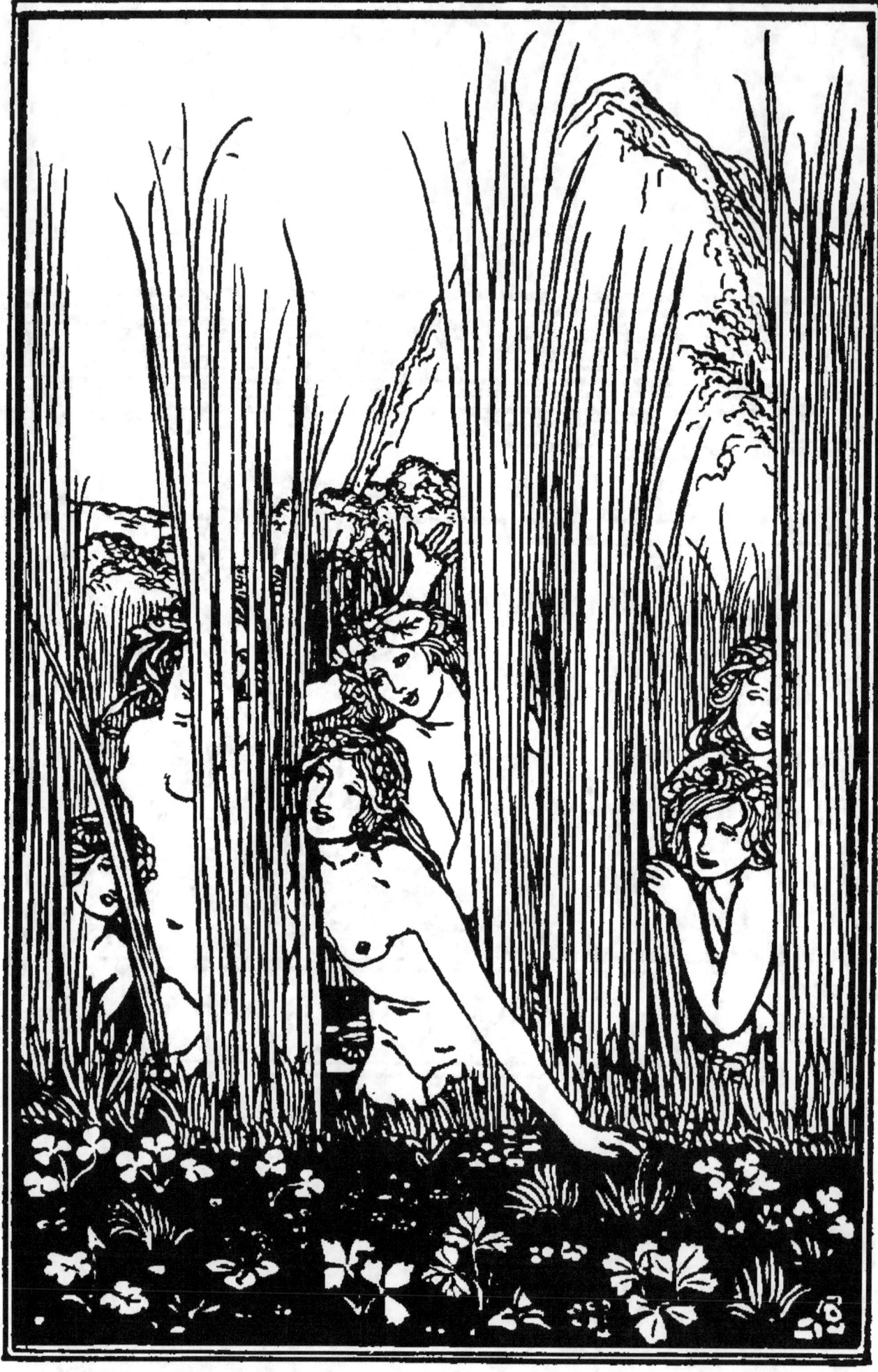

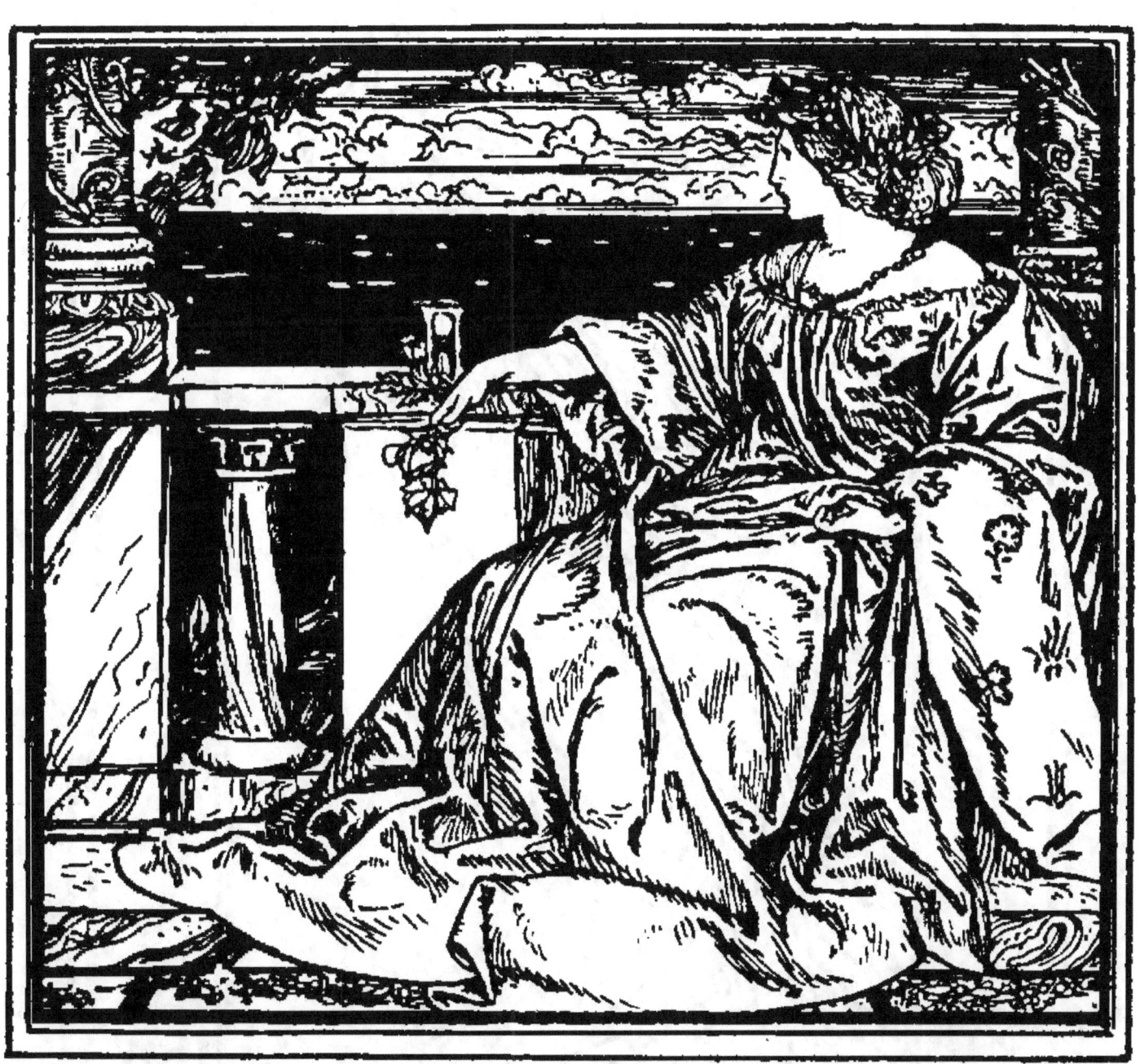

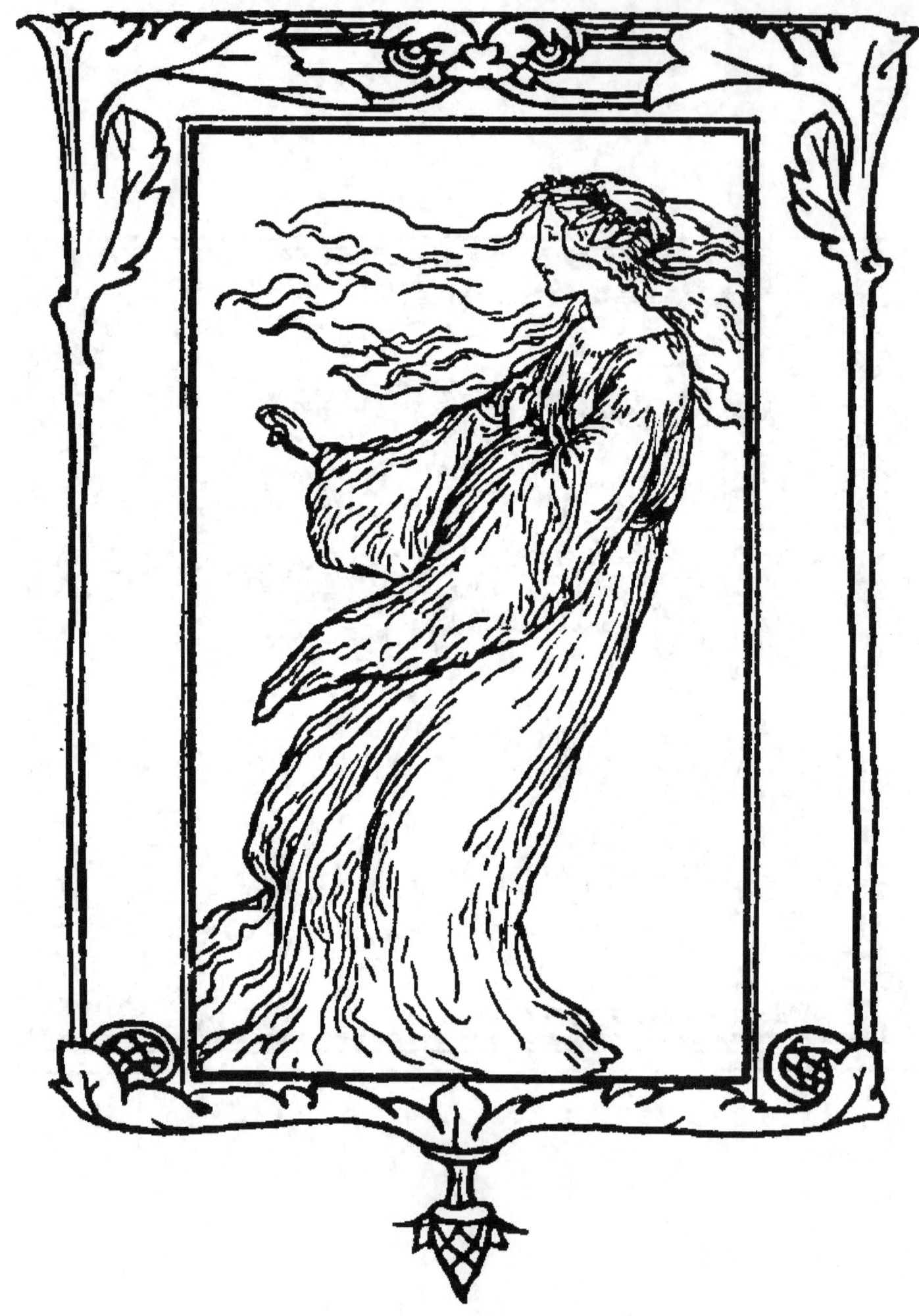

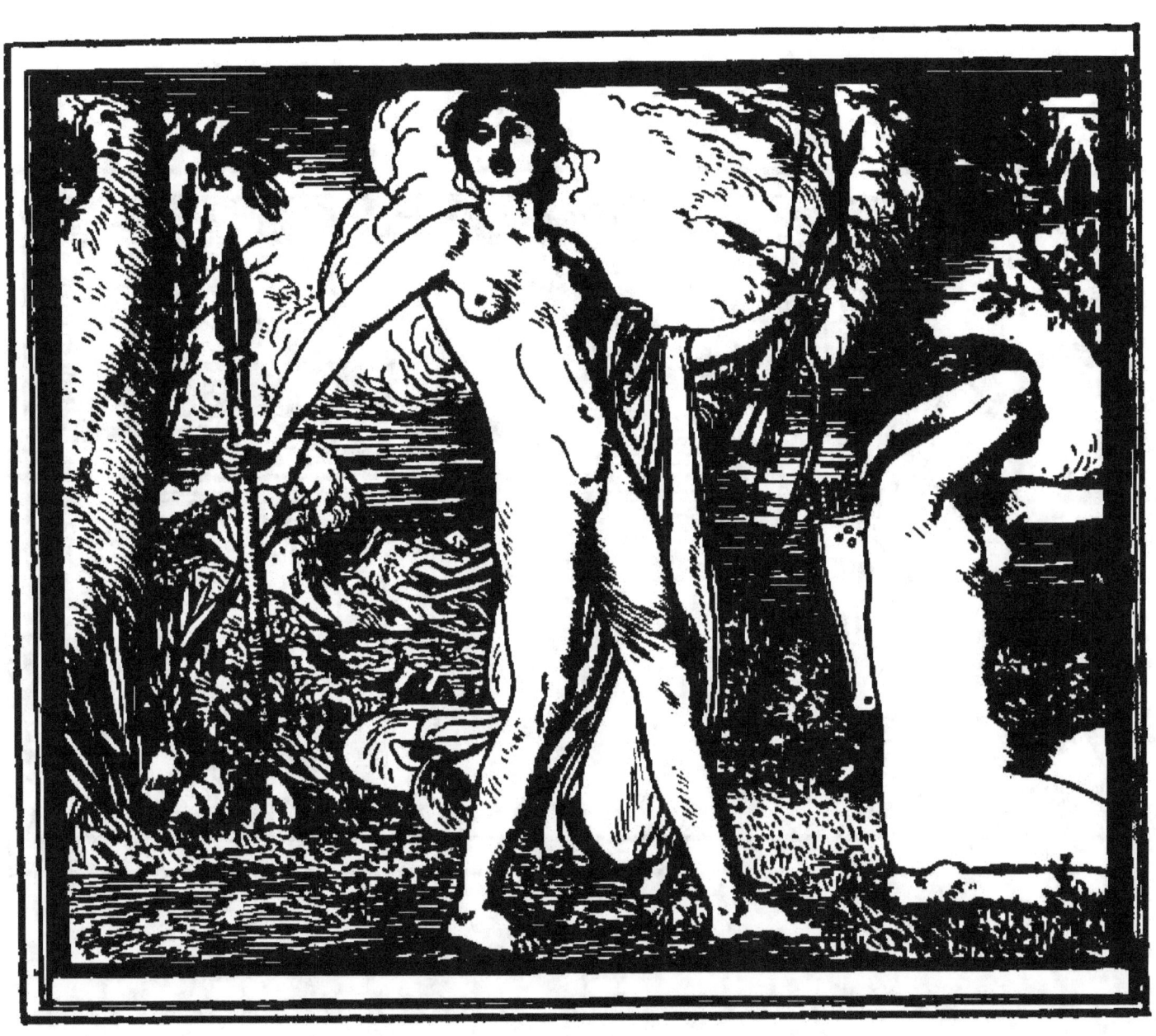

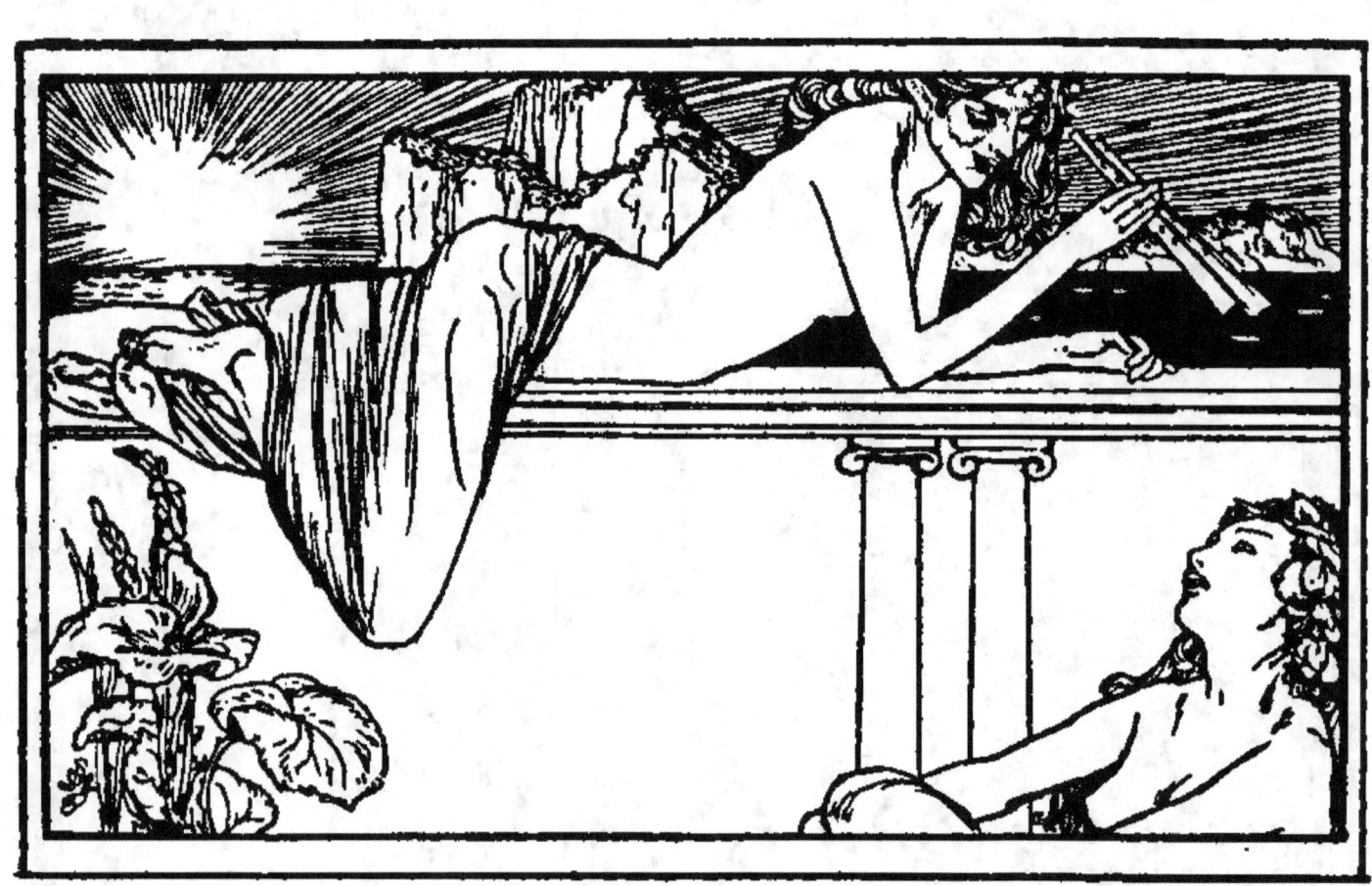

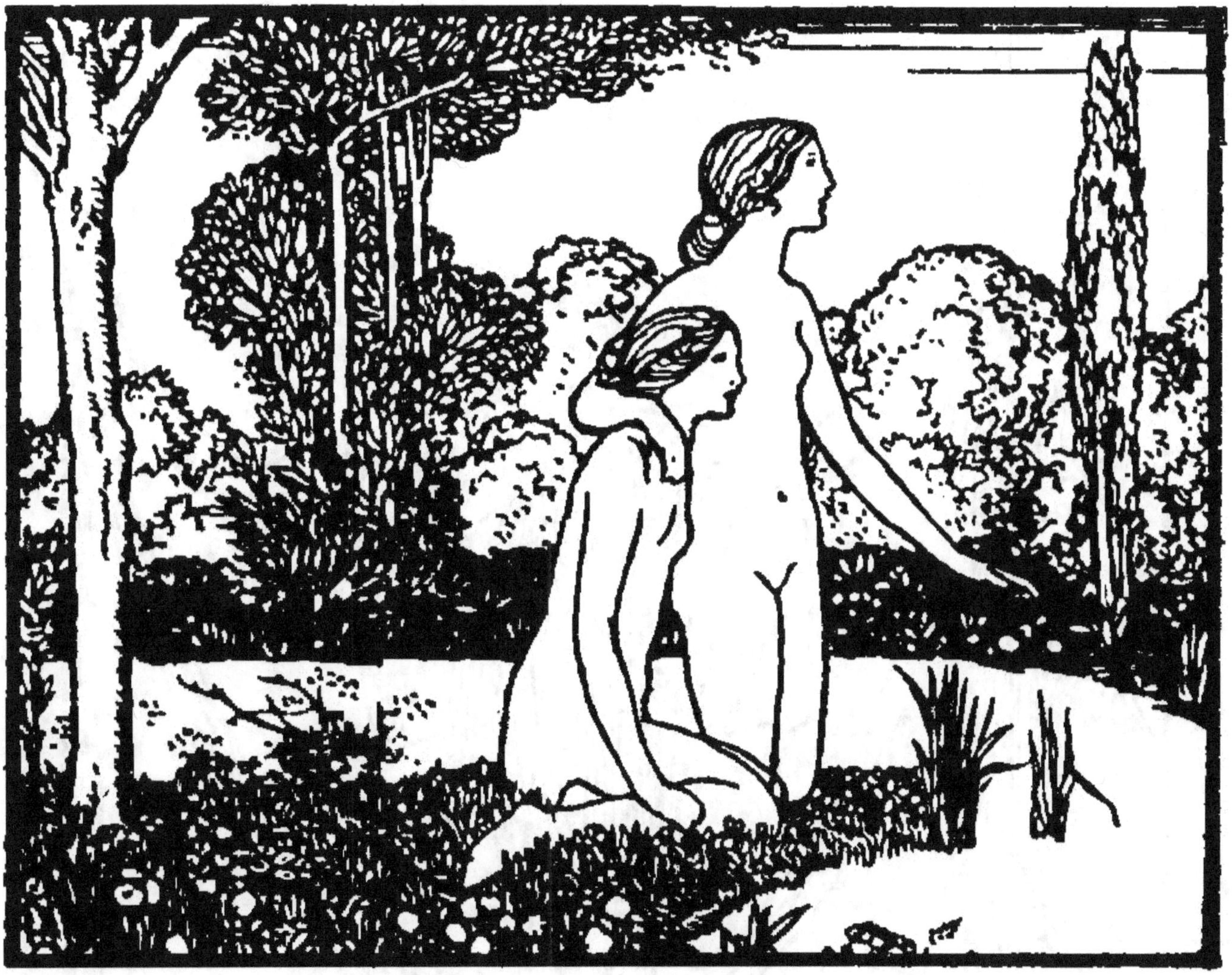

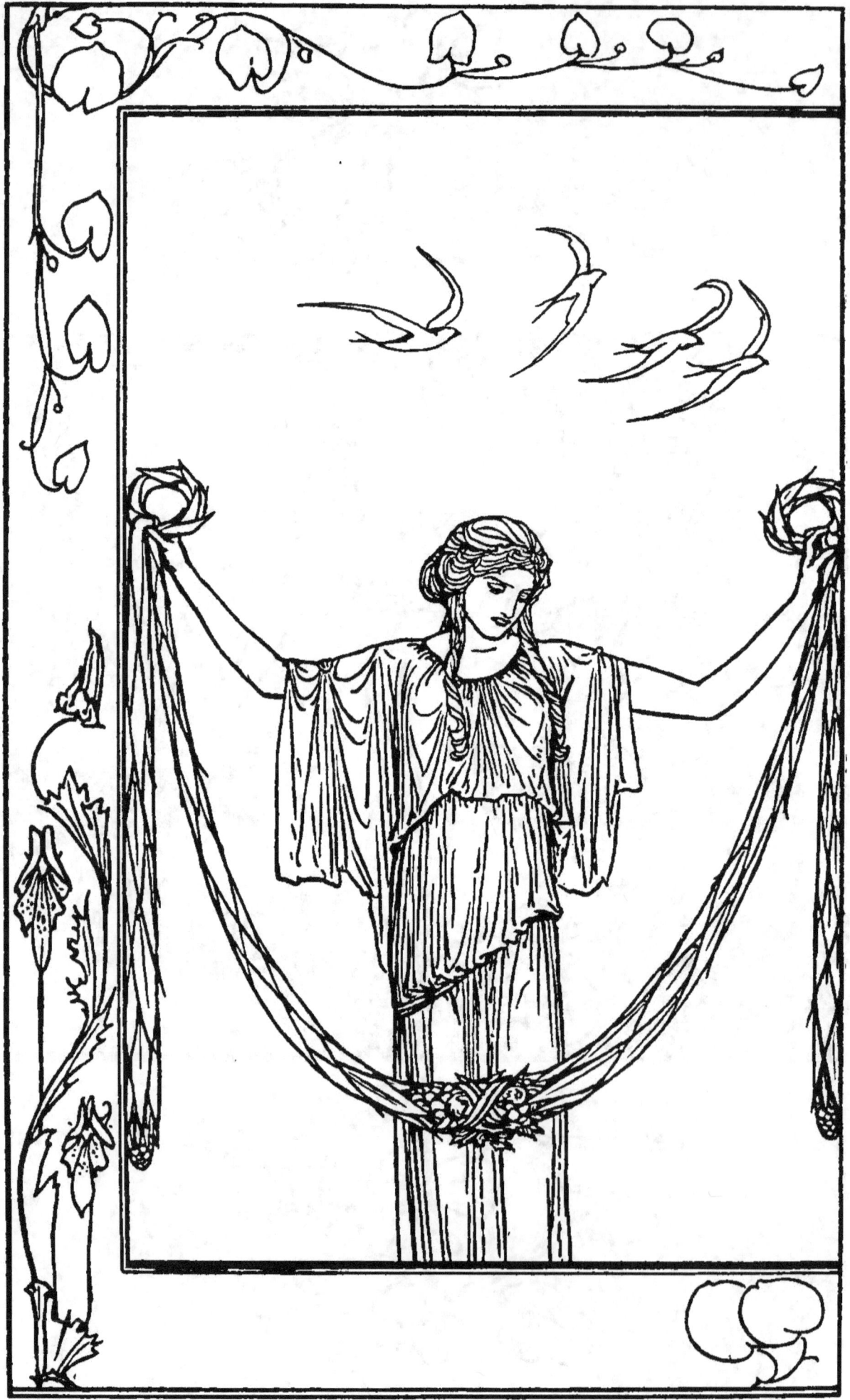

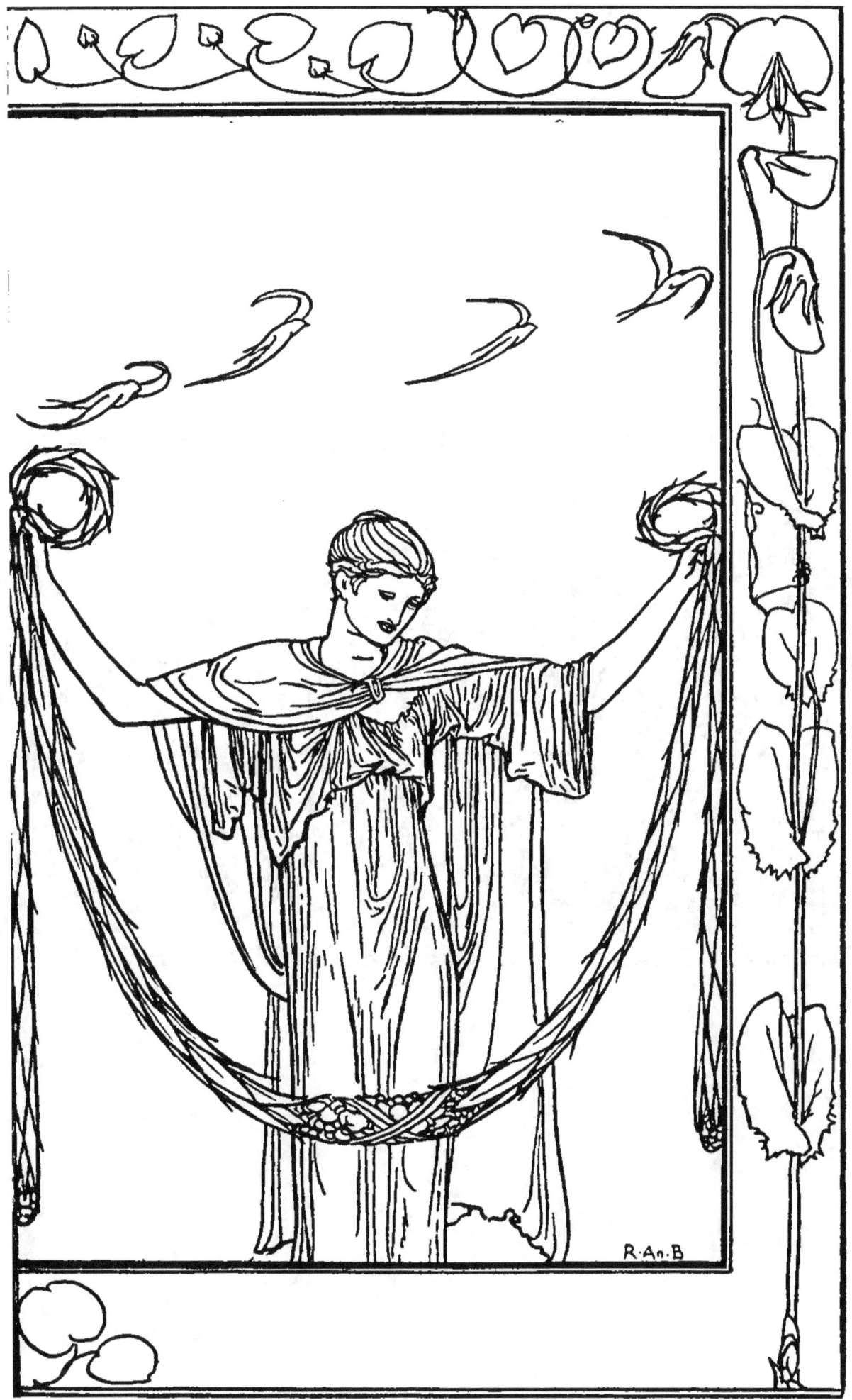

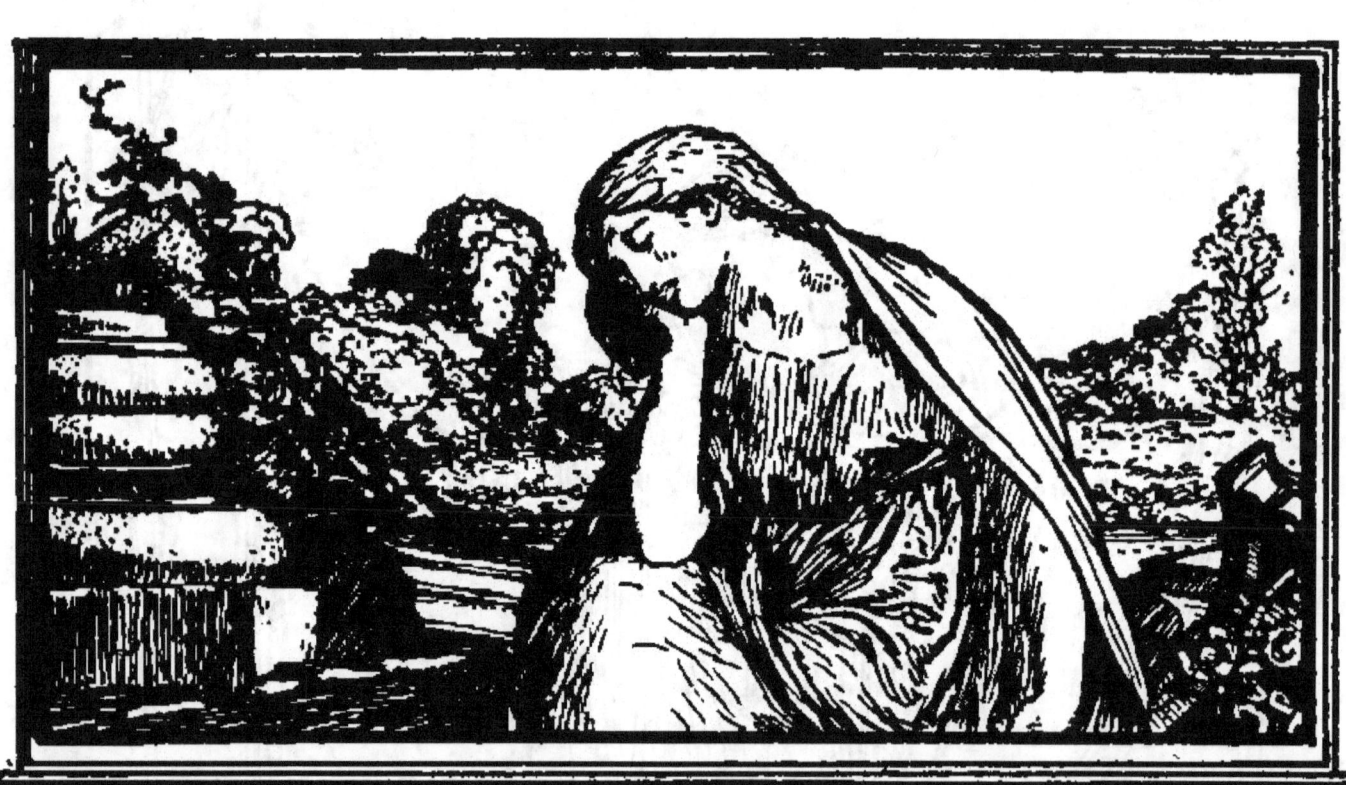

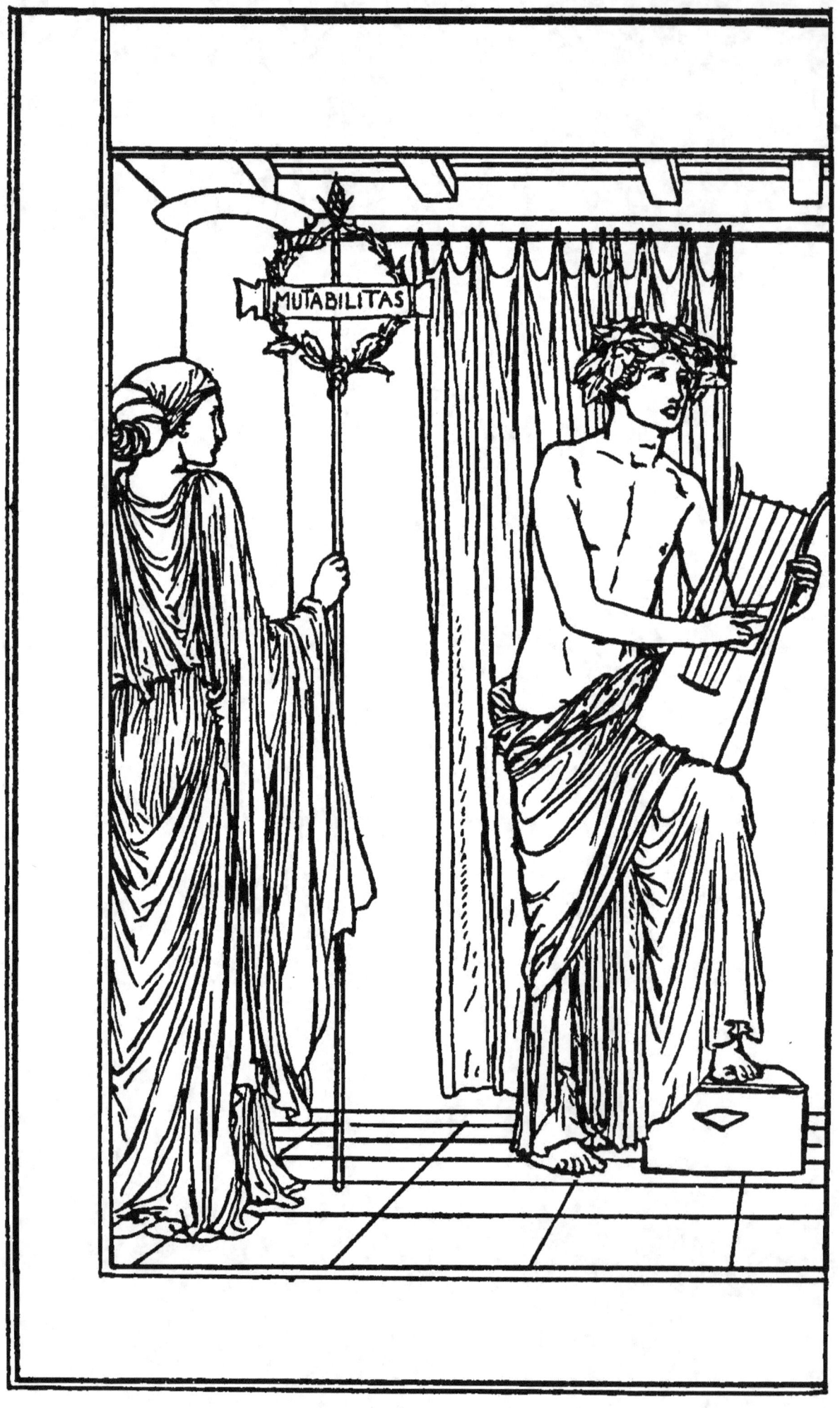

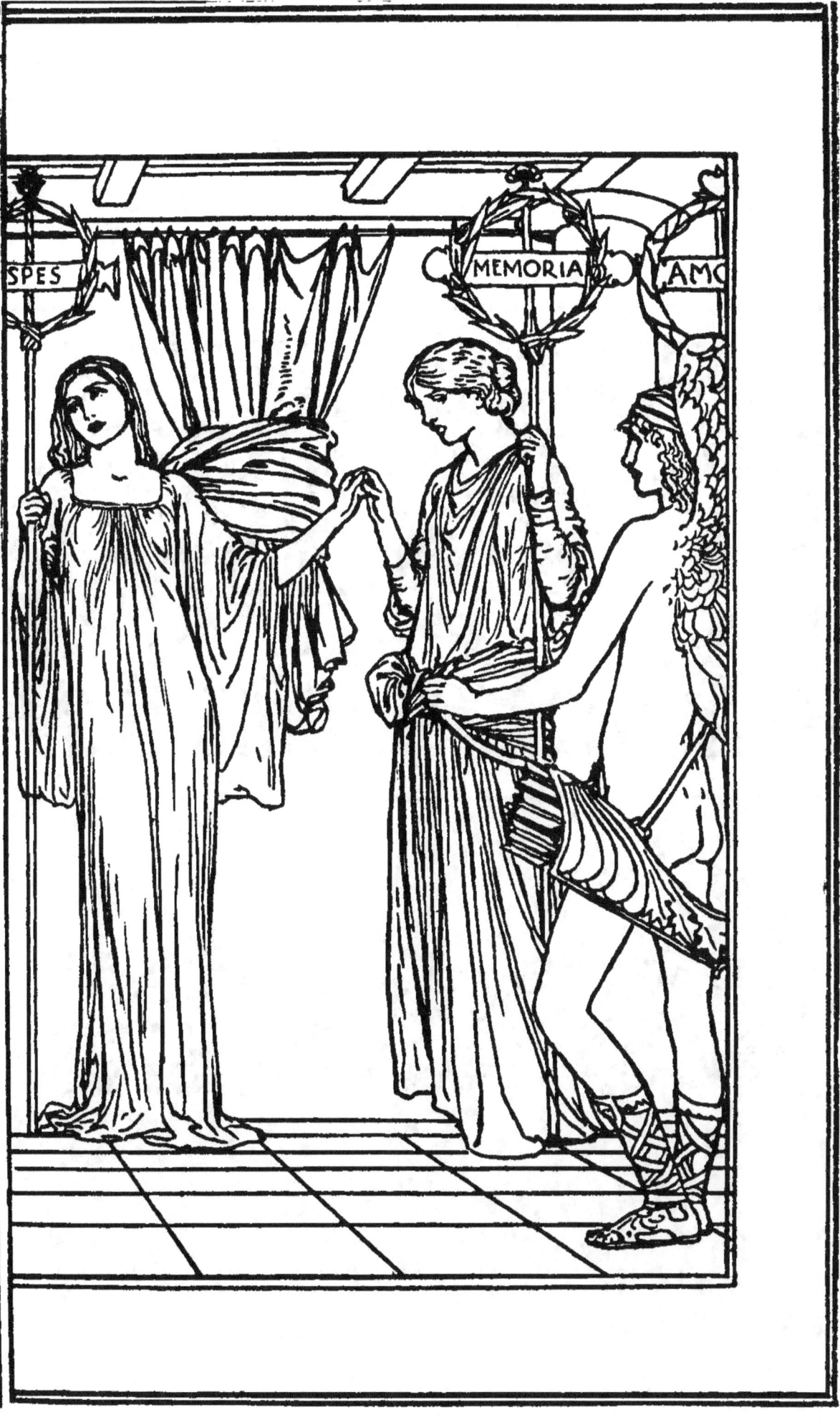

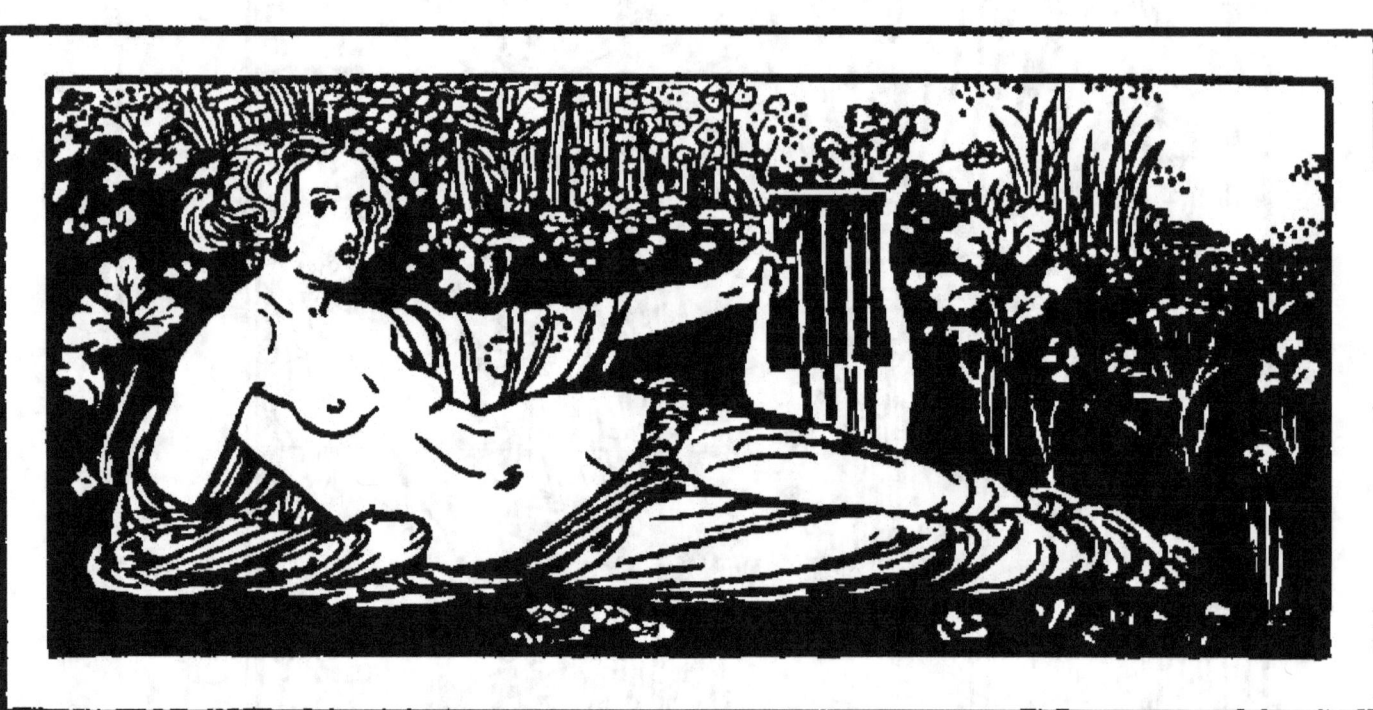

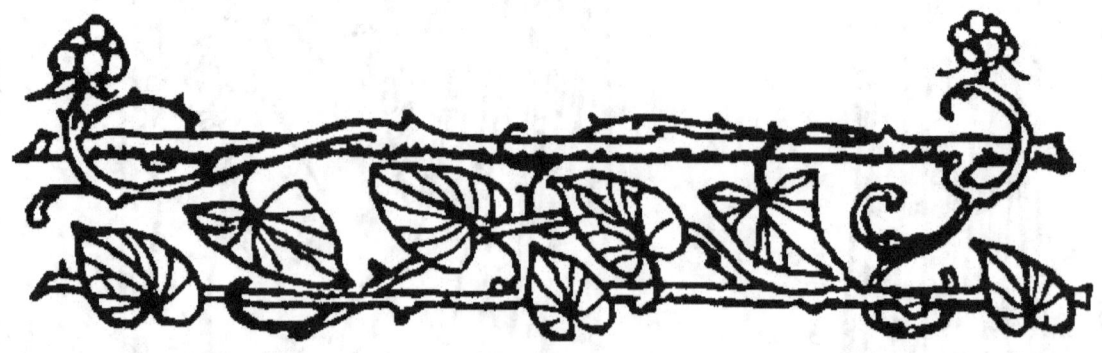

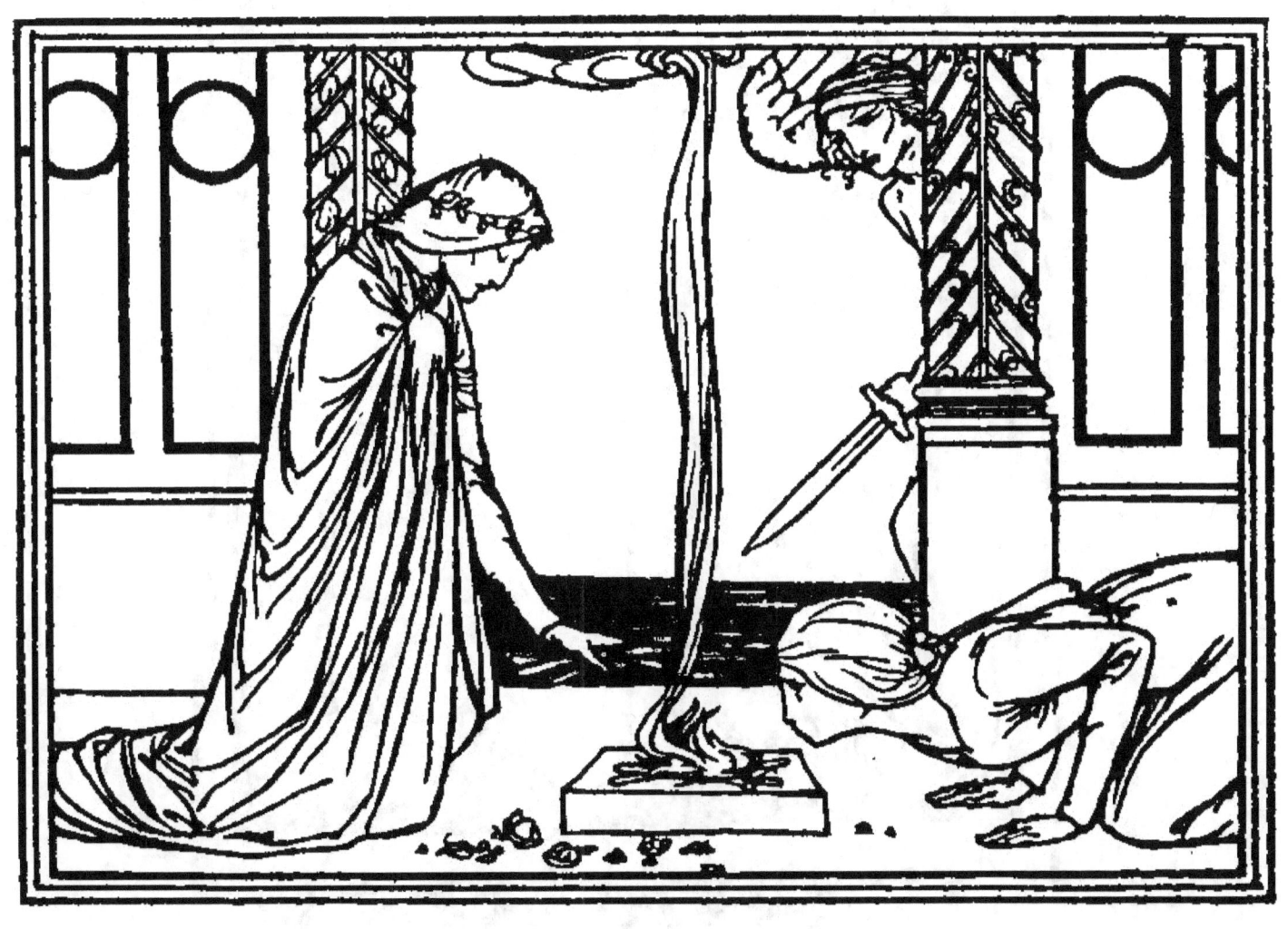

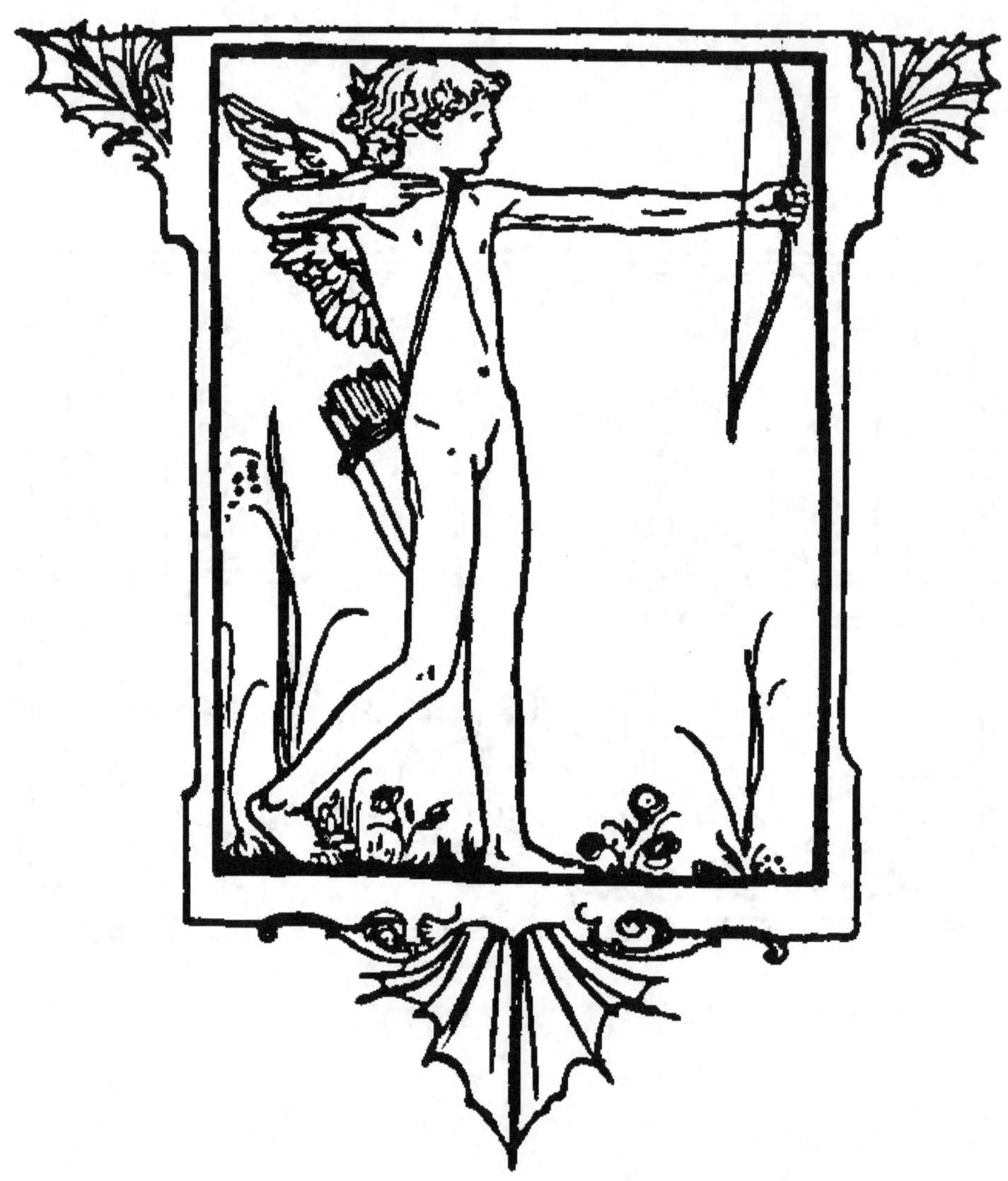

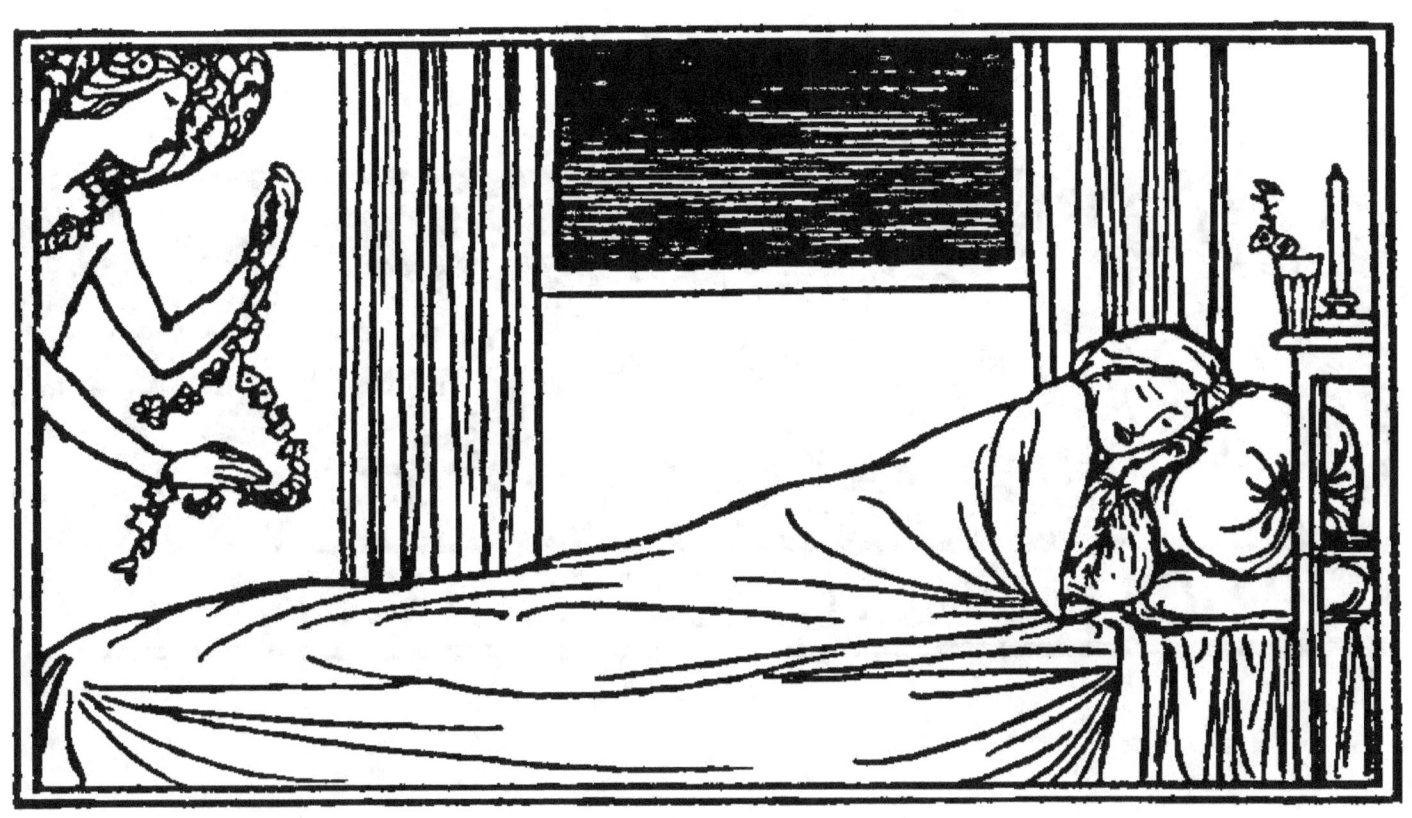

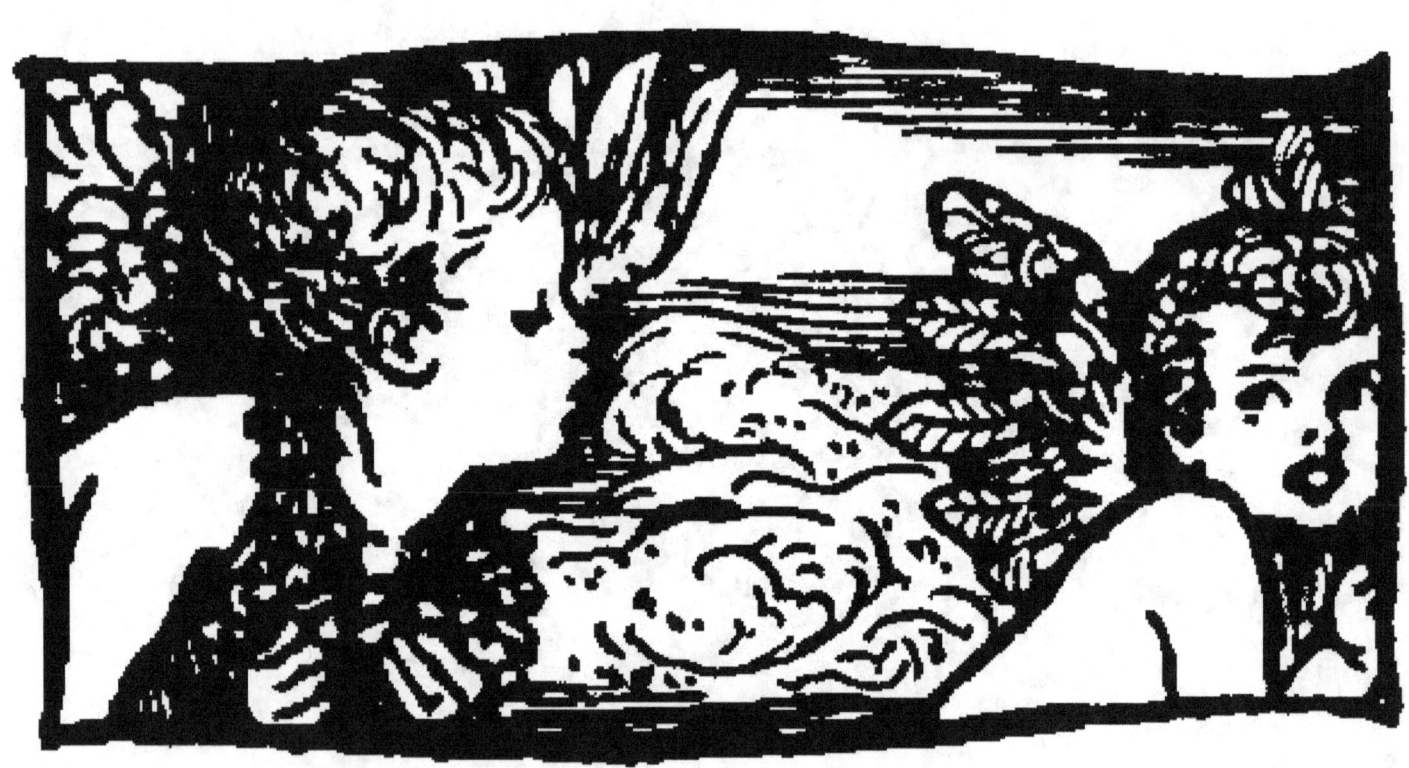

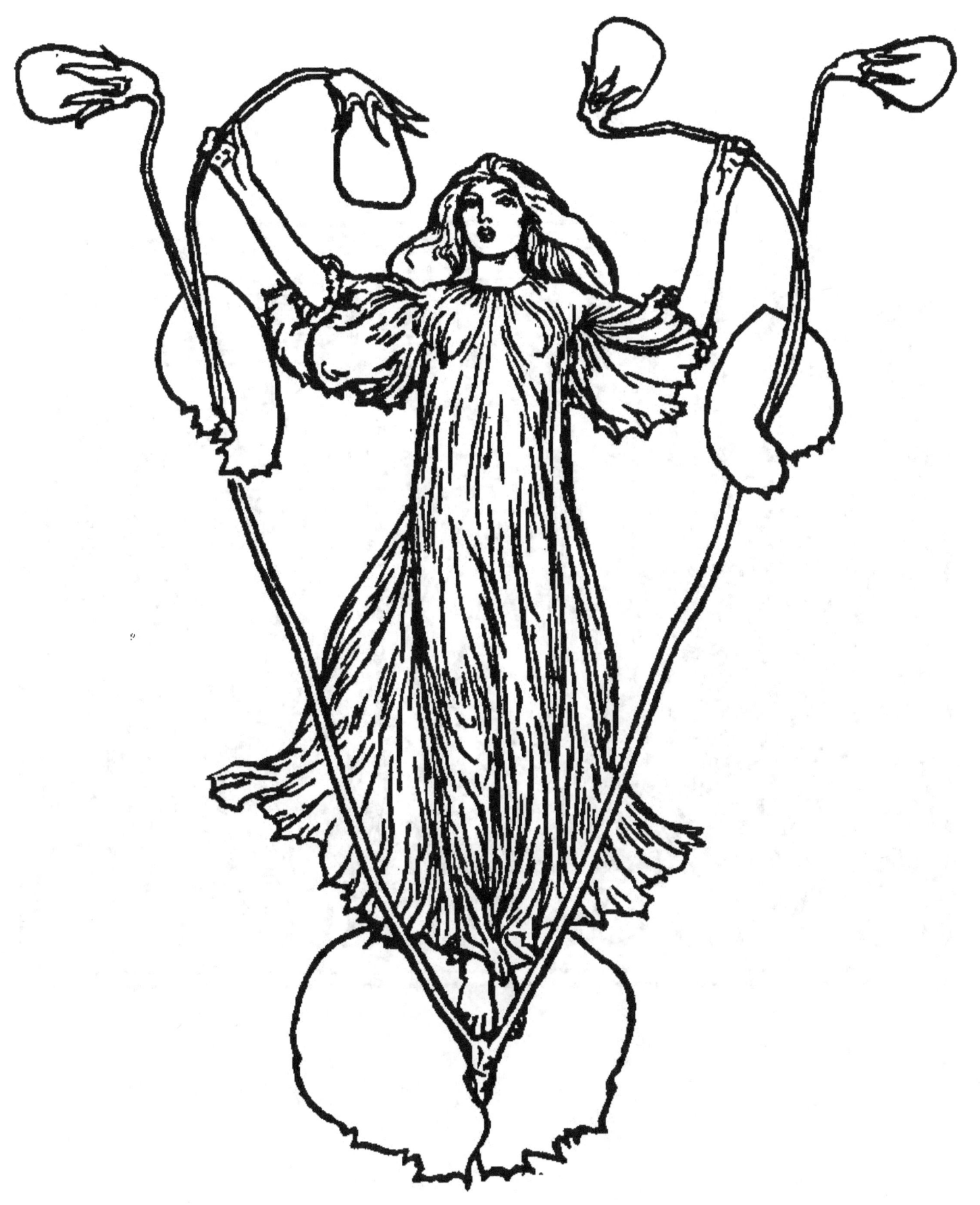

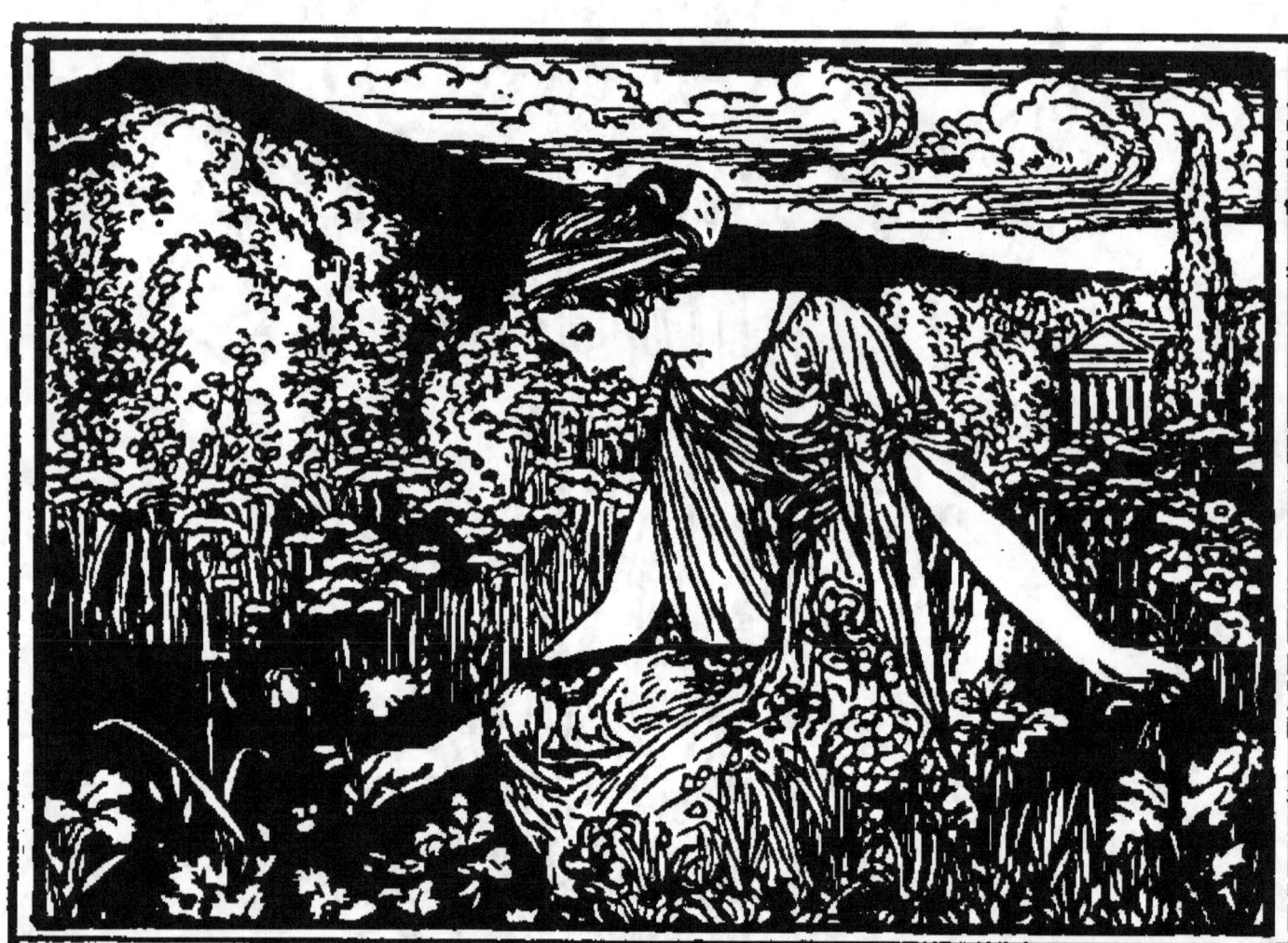

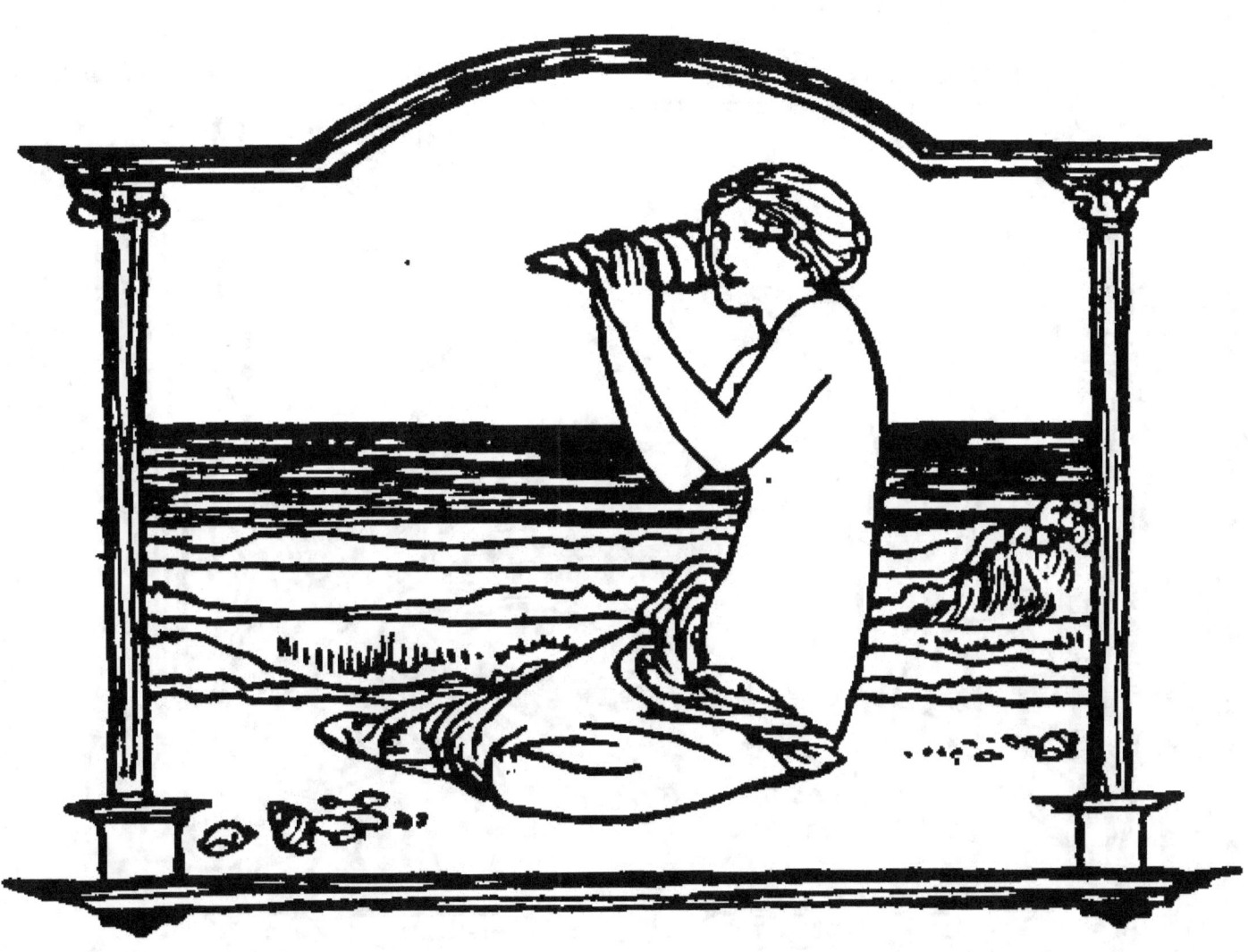

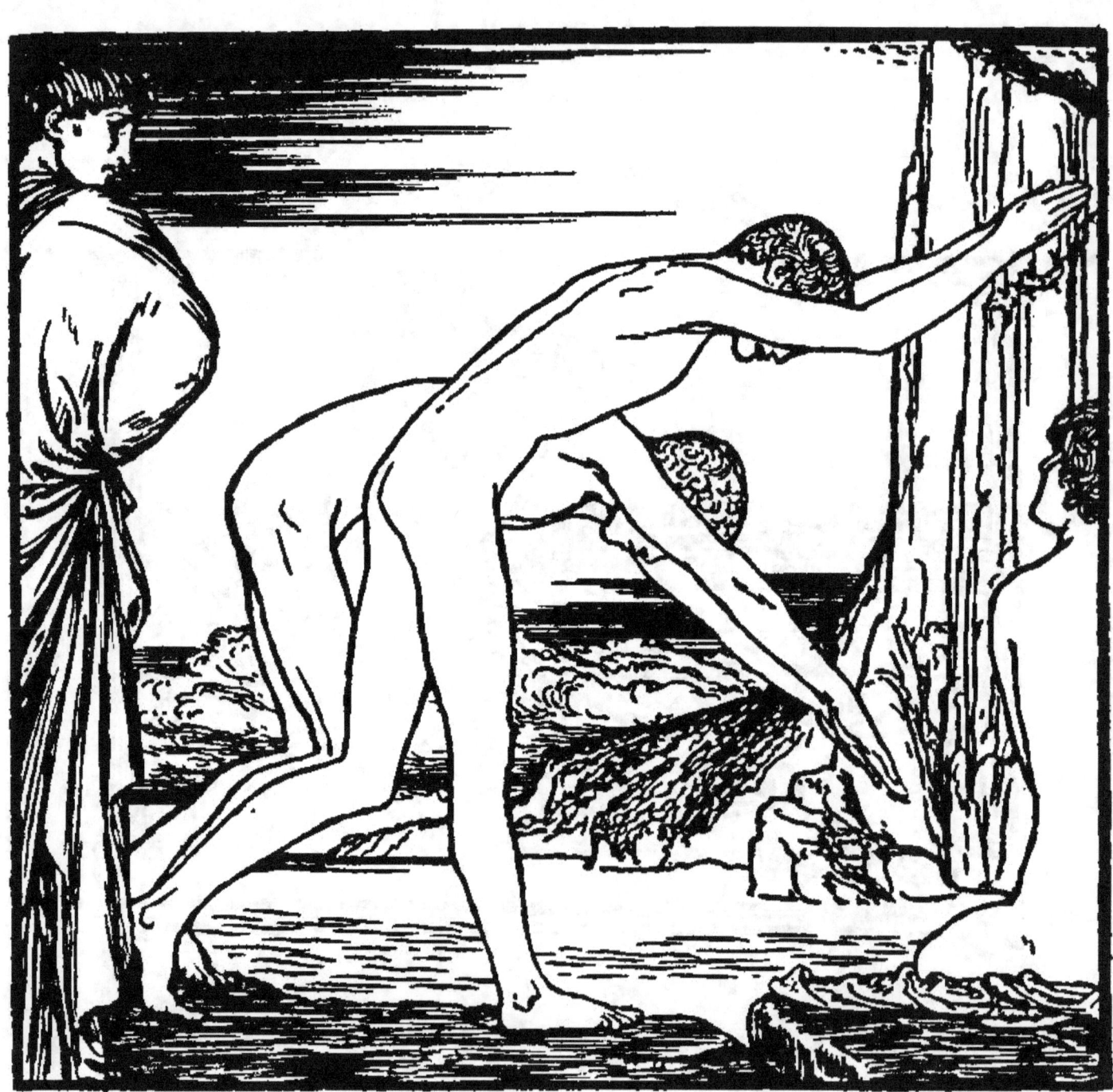

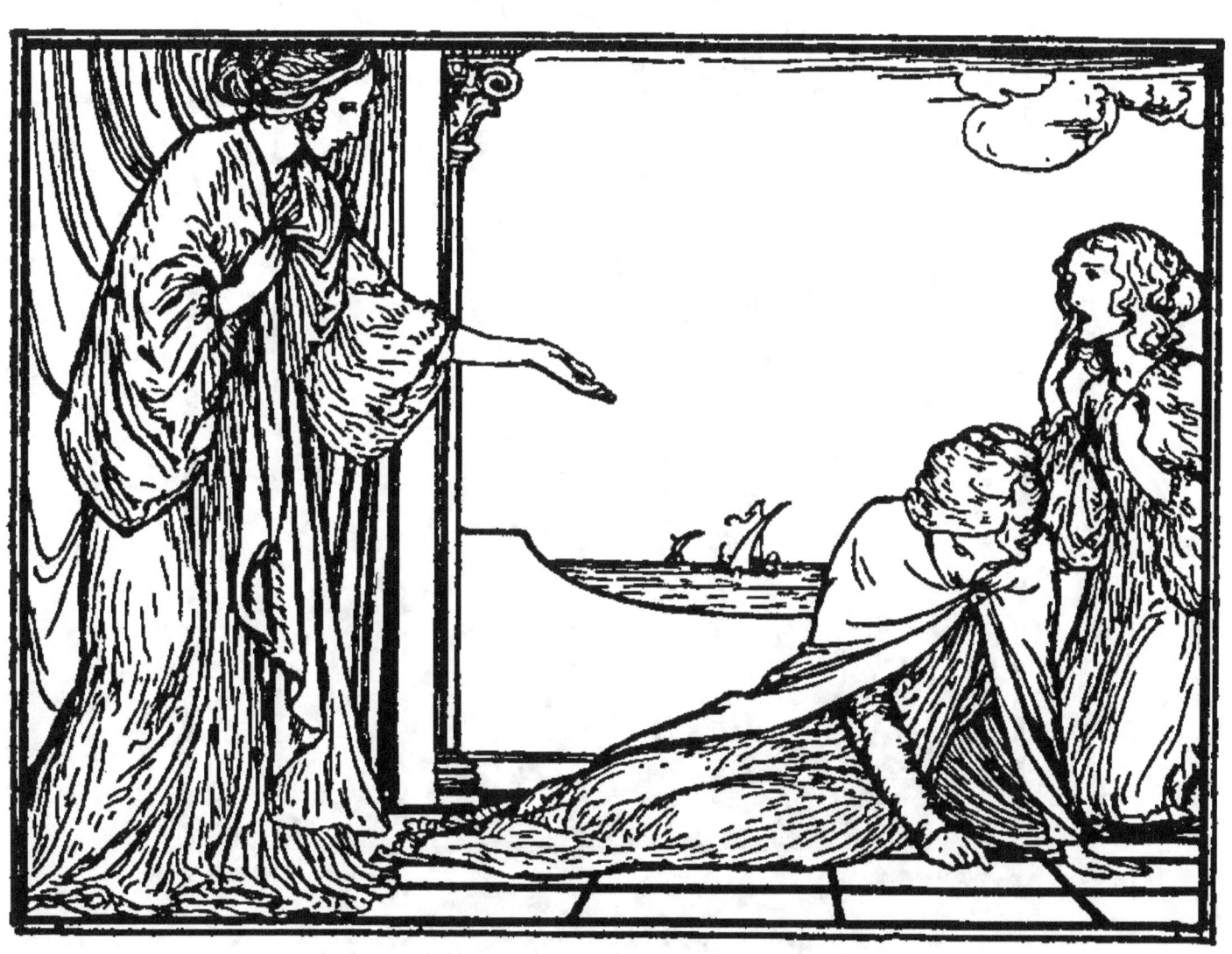

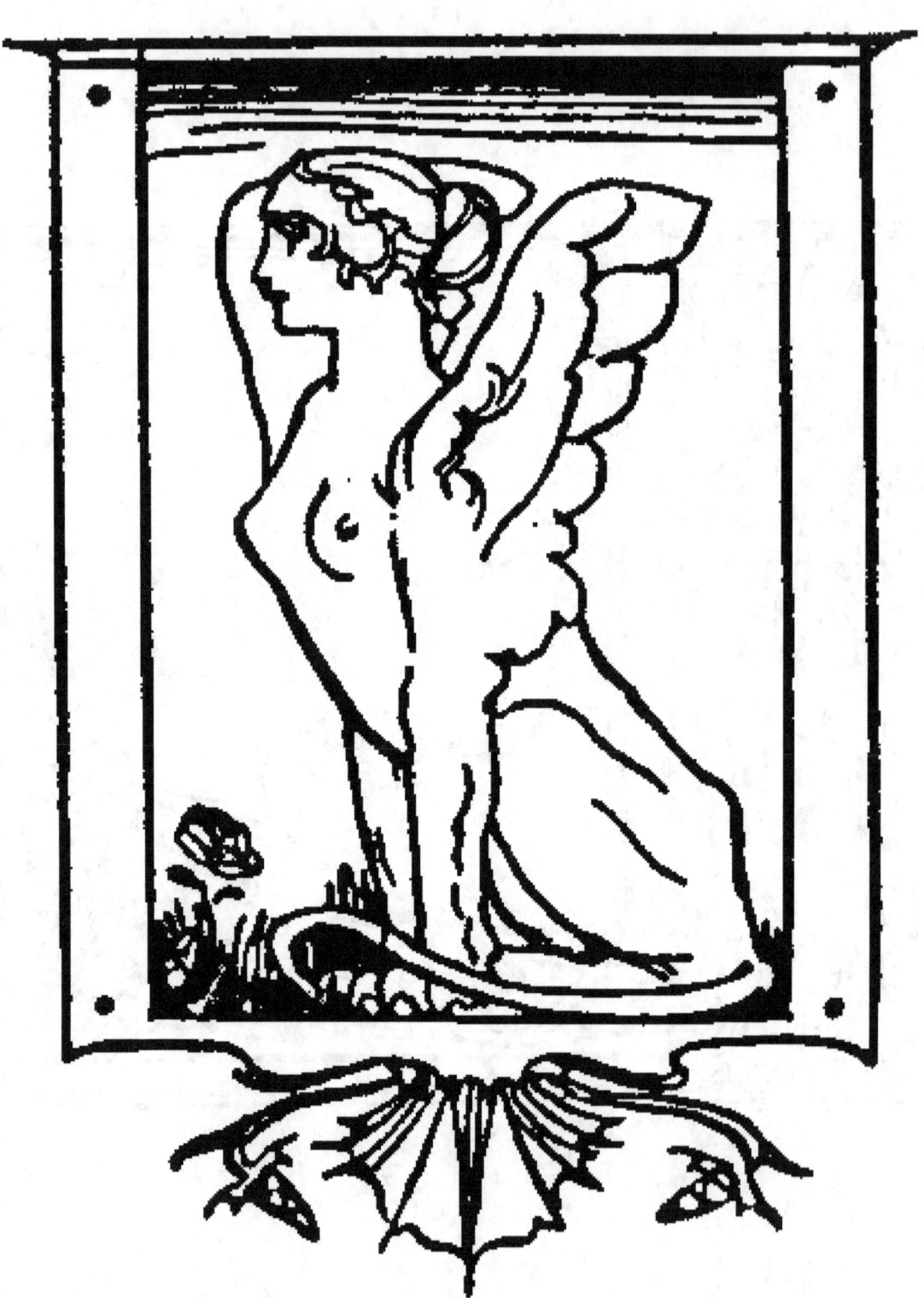

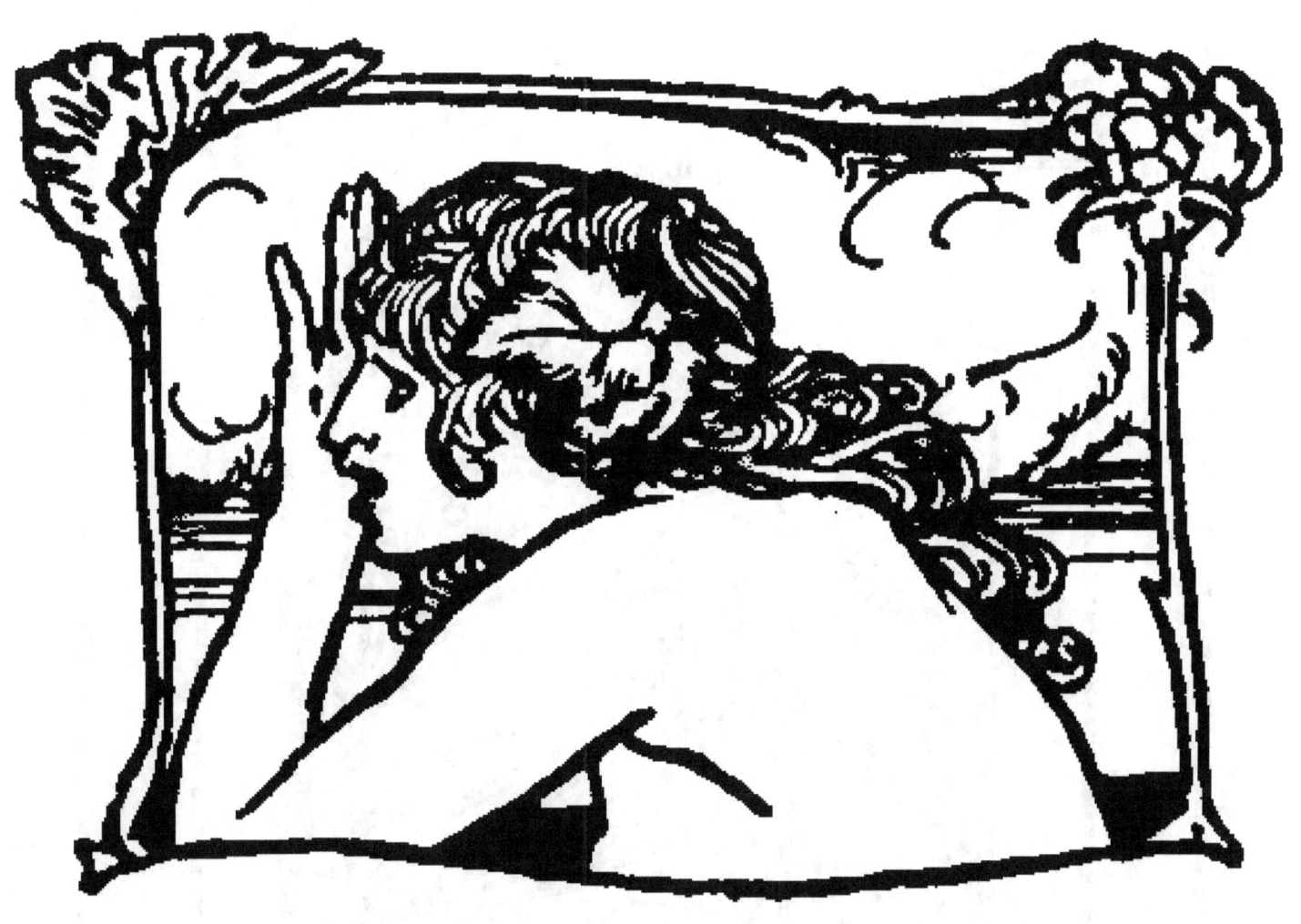

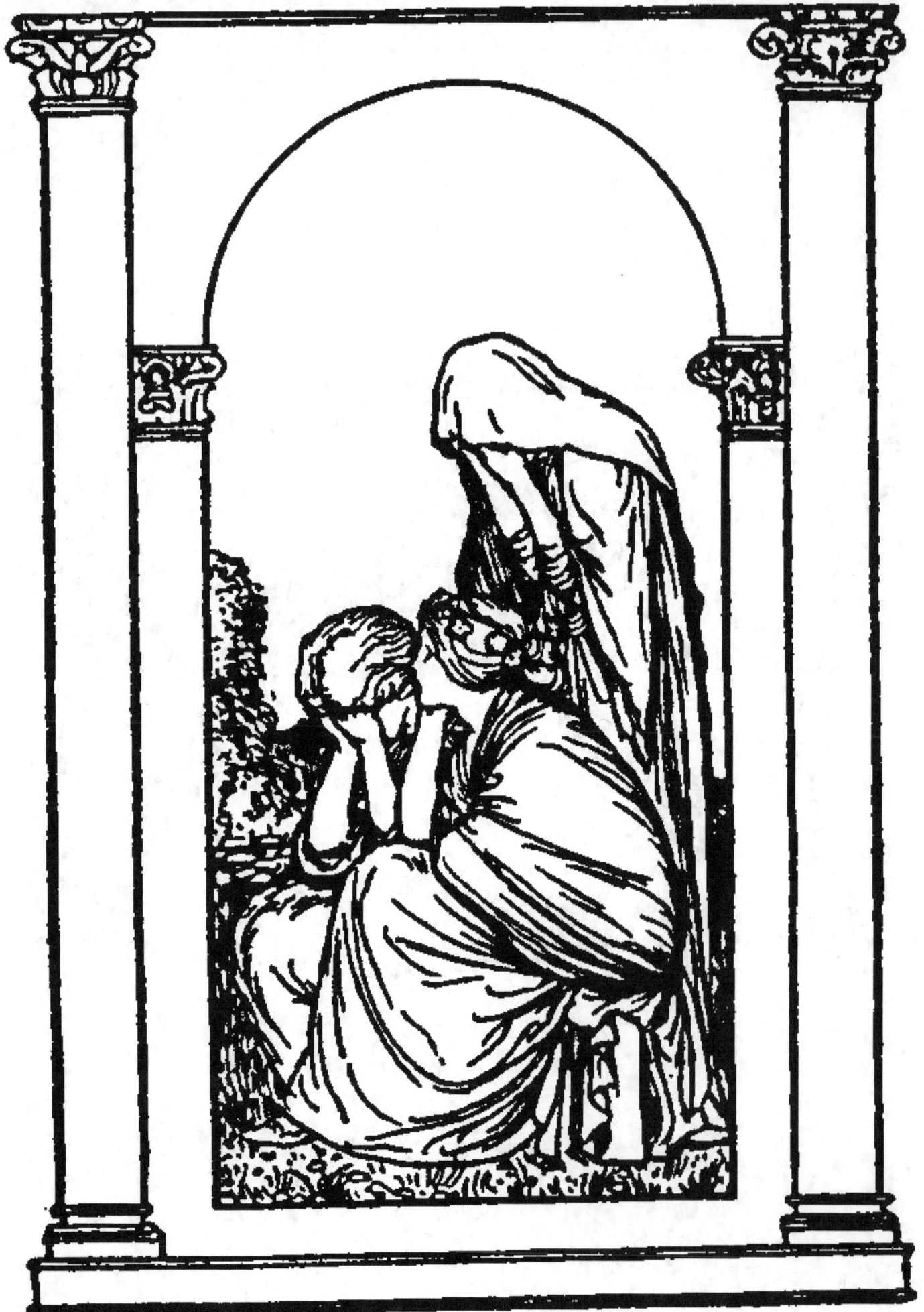

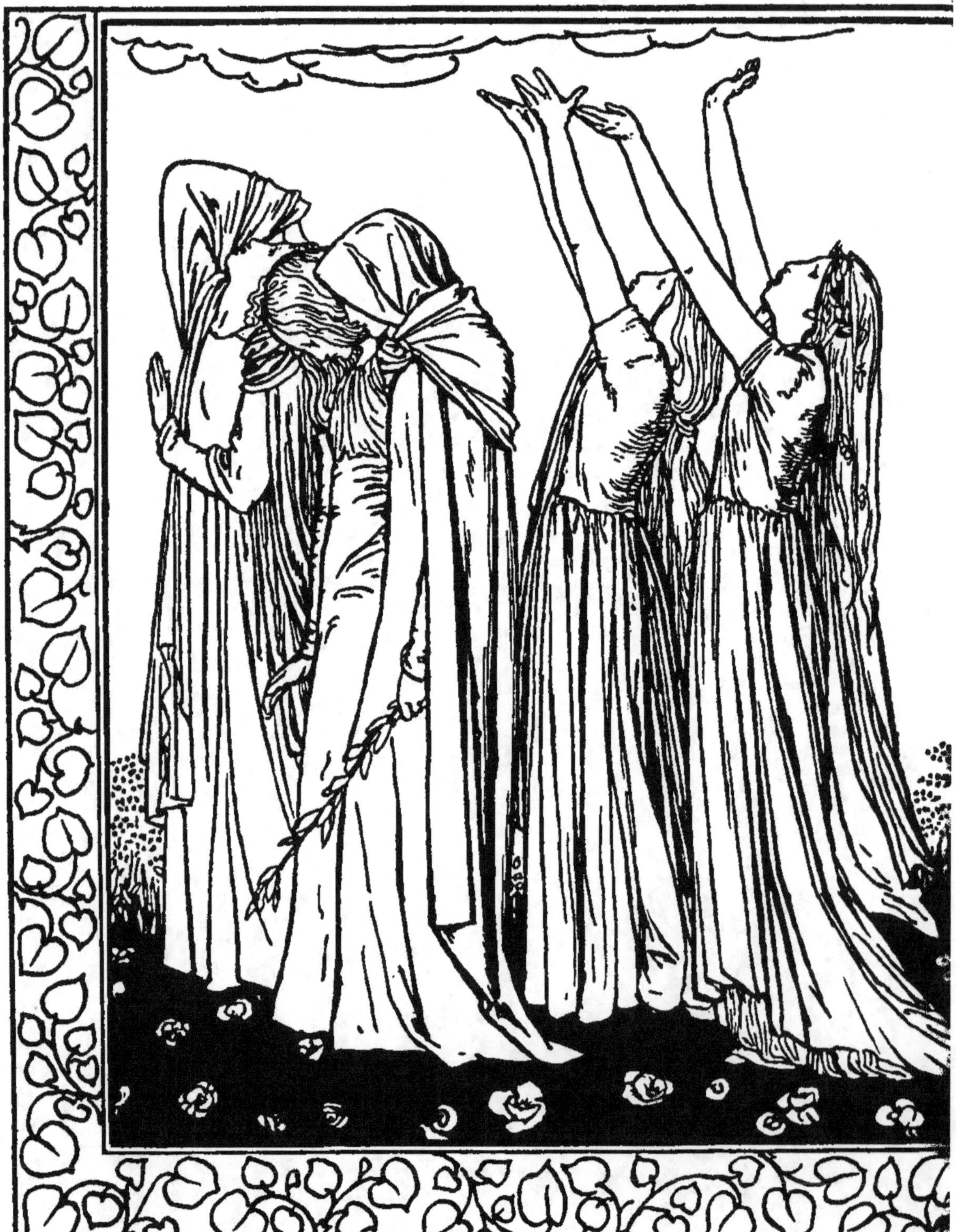

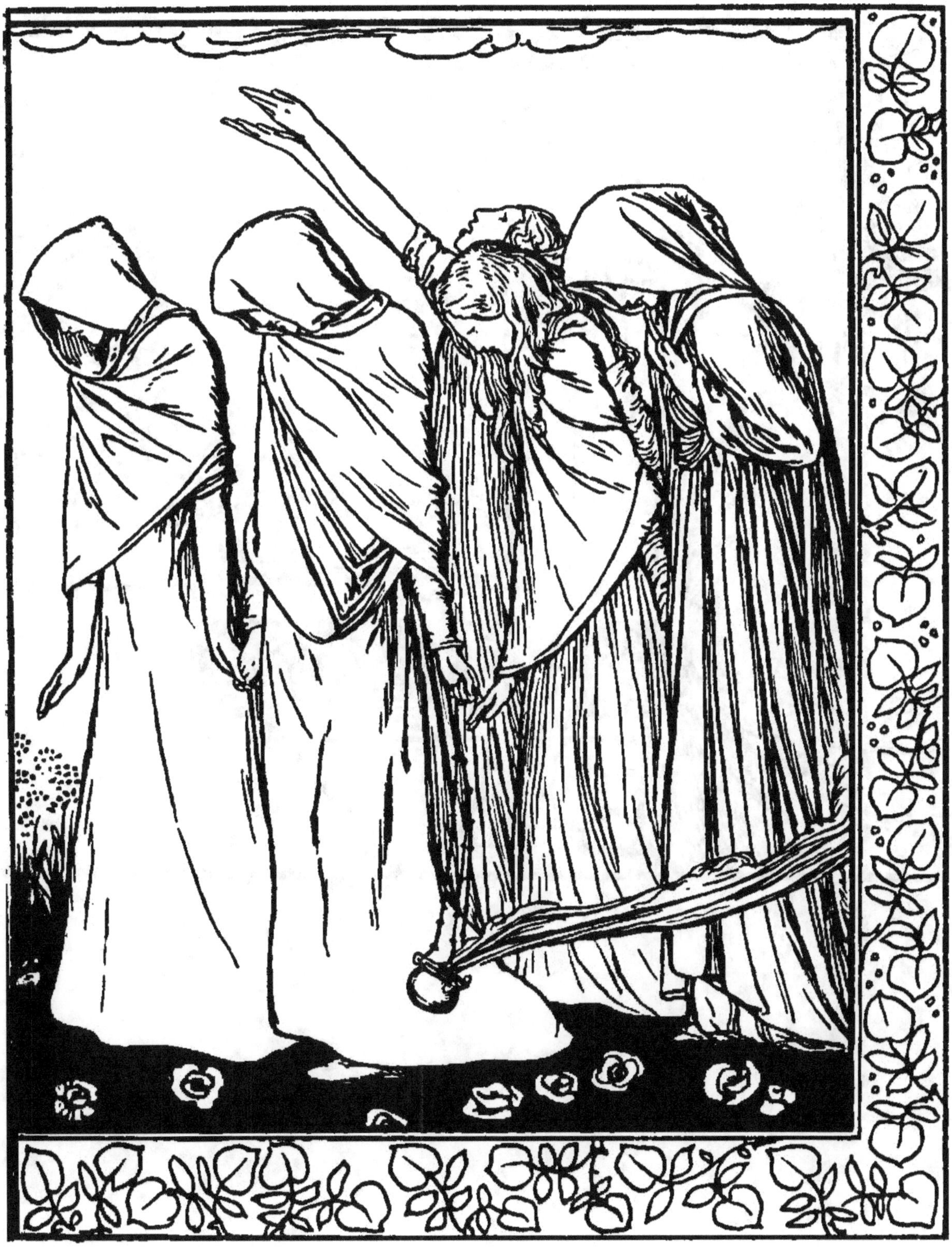

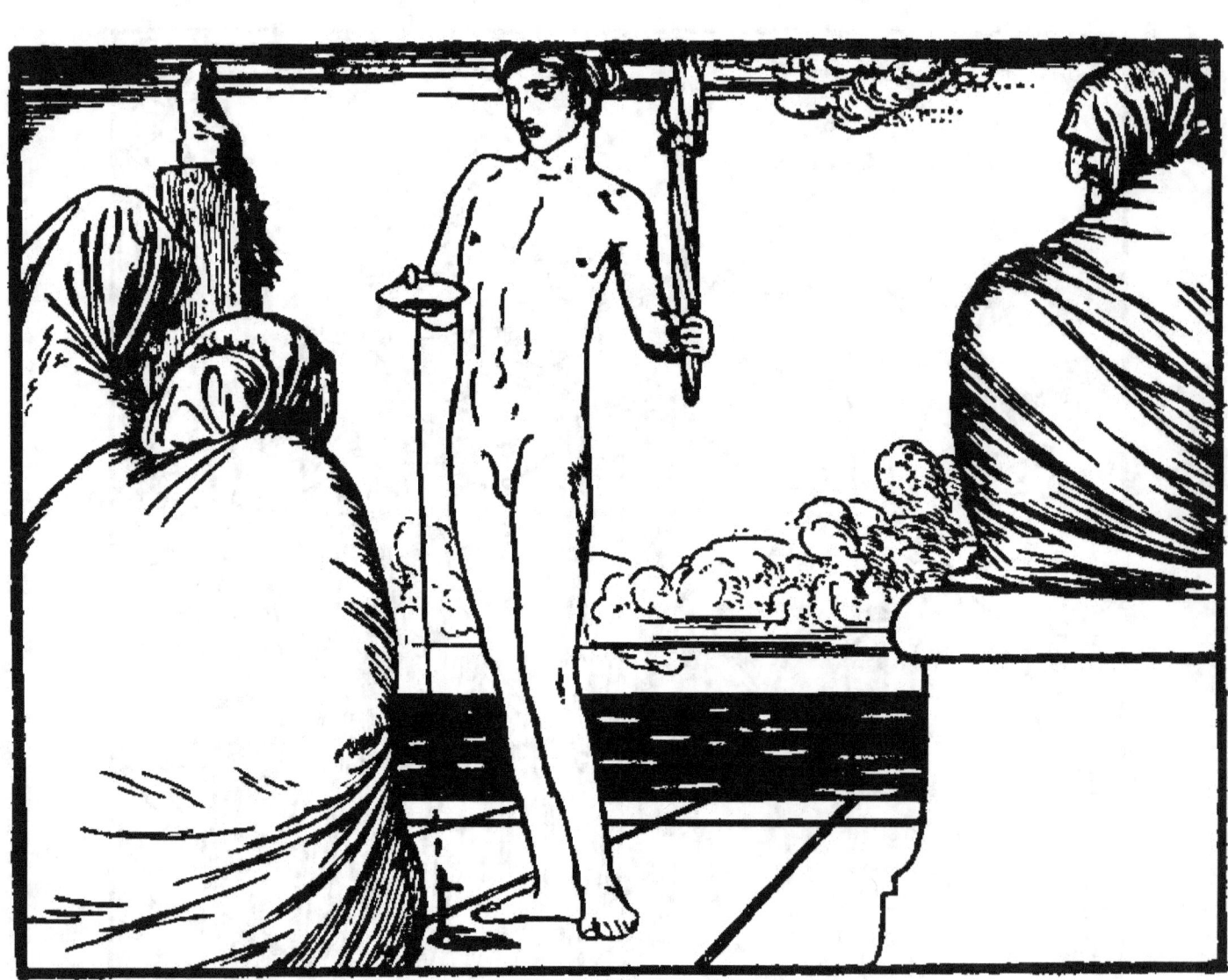

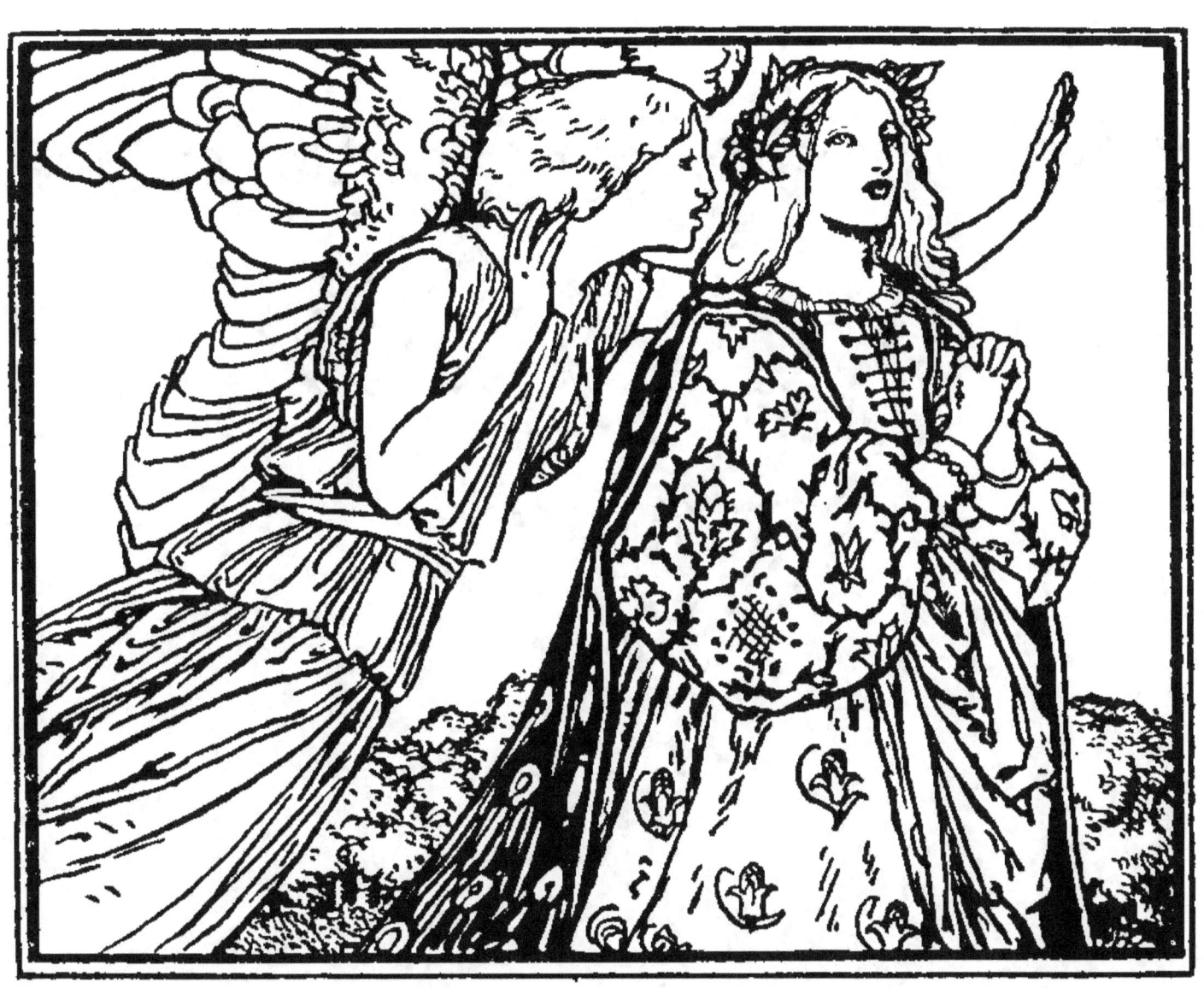

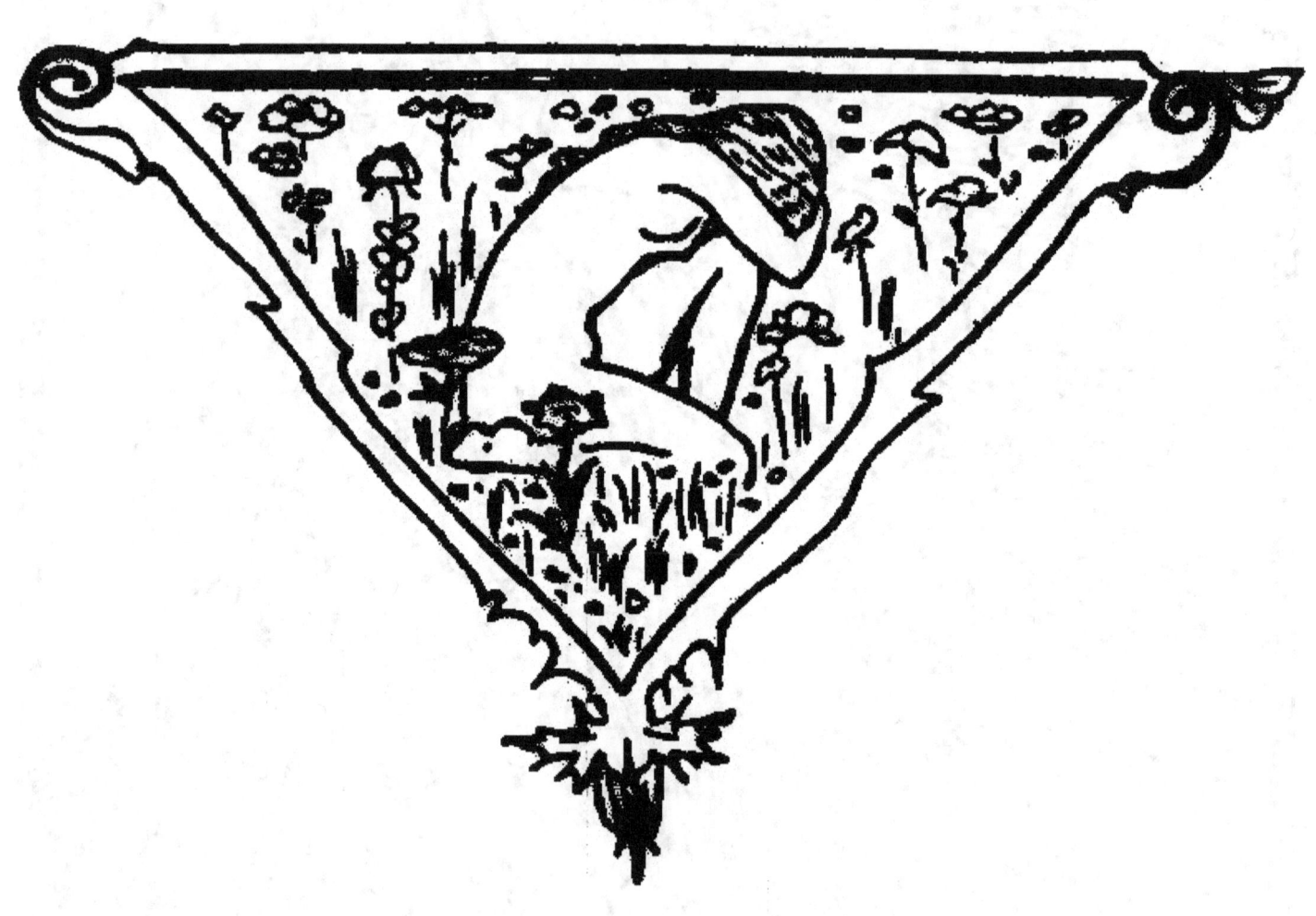

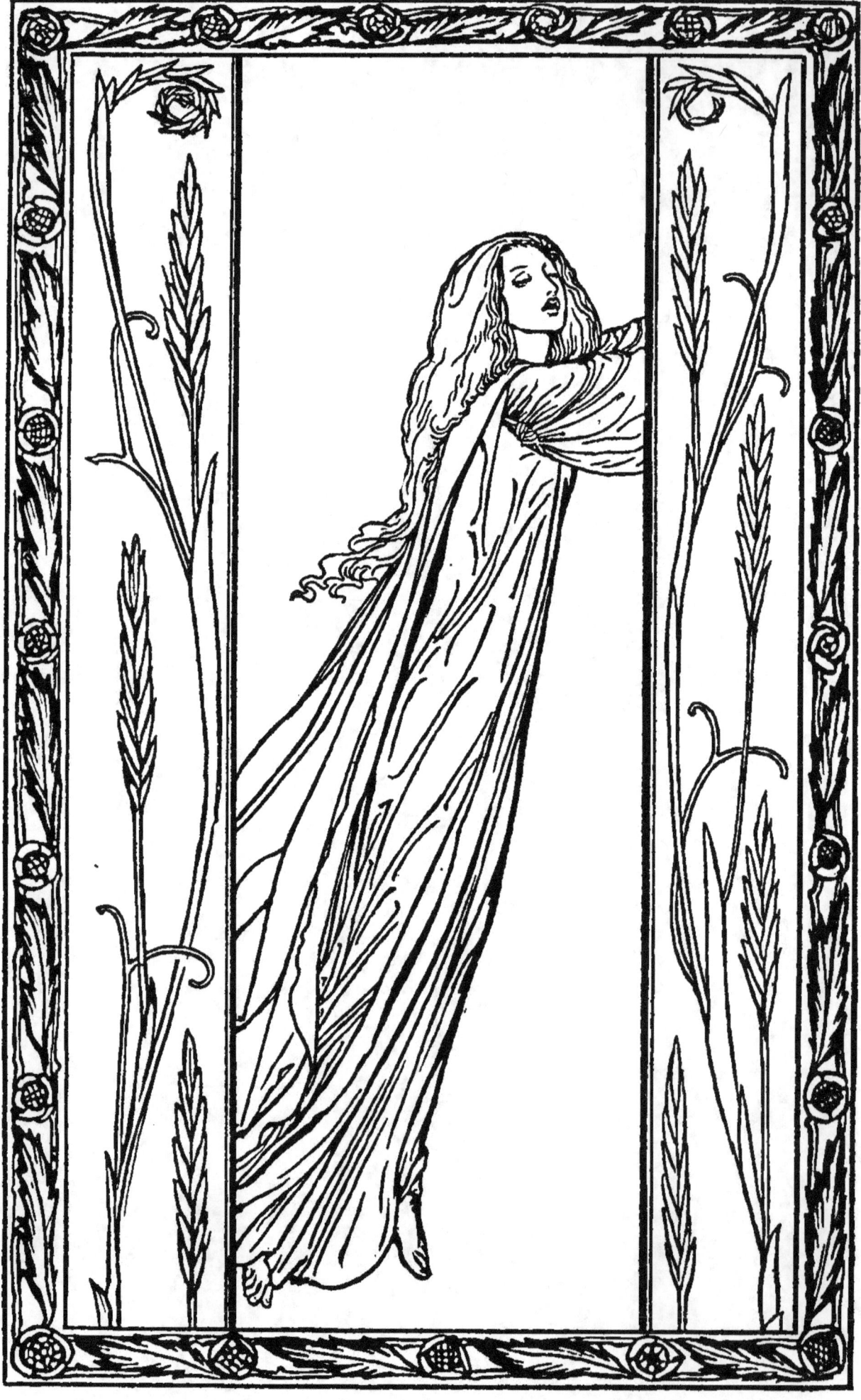

EPIPSYCHIDION

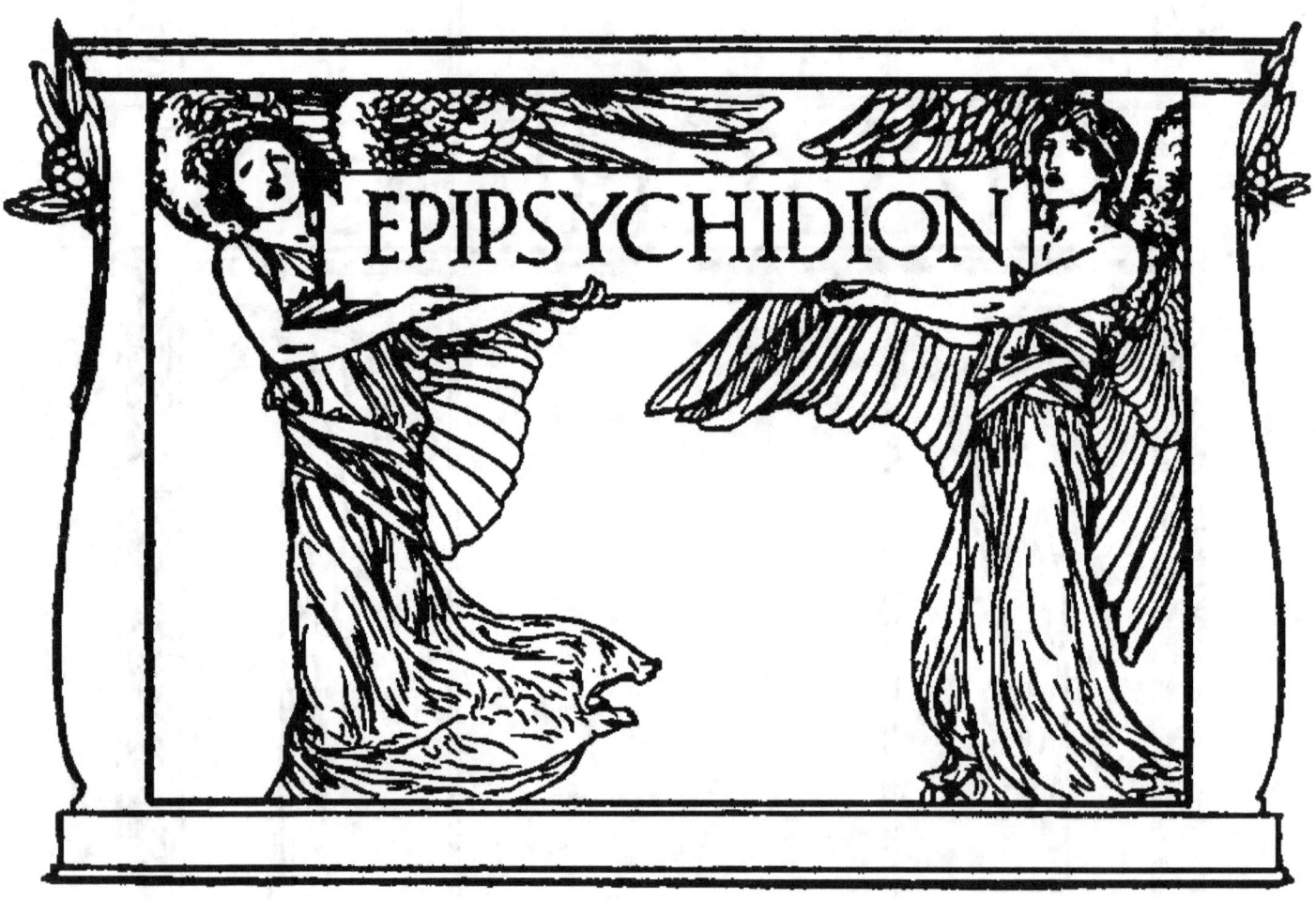

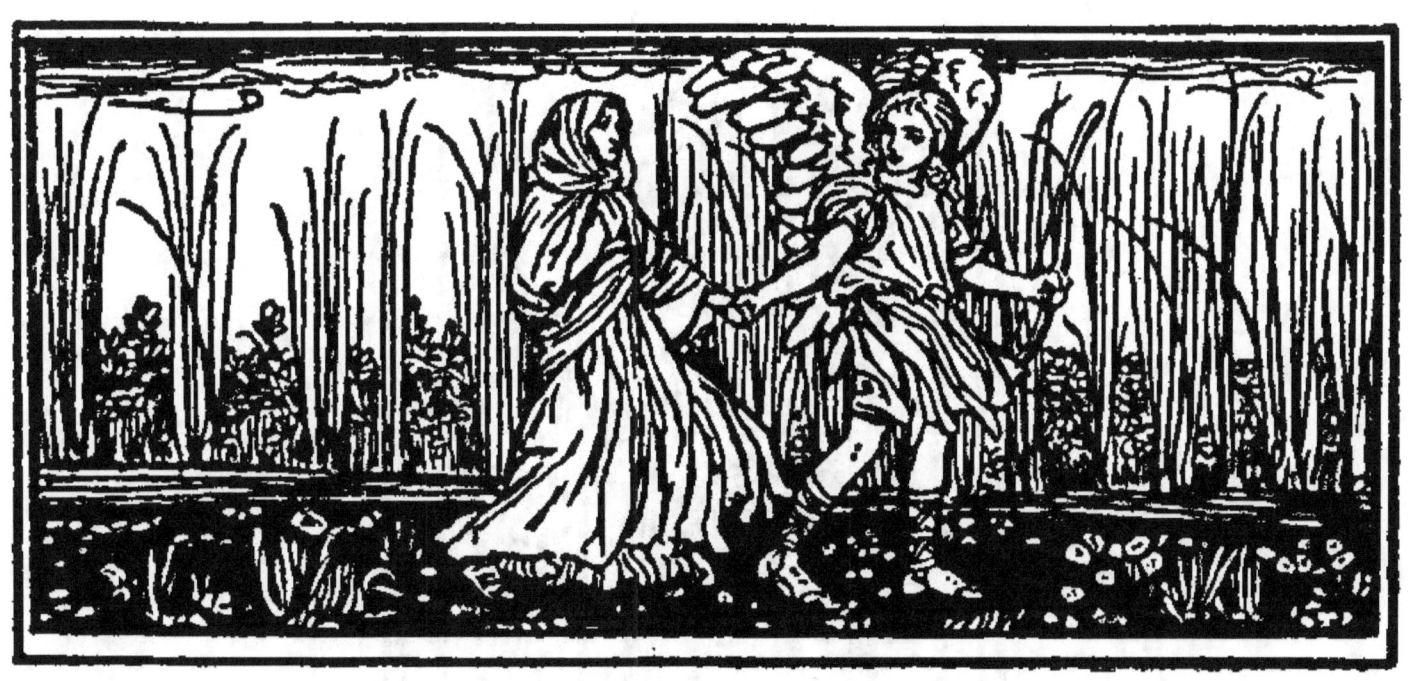

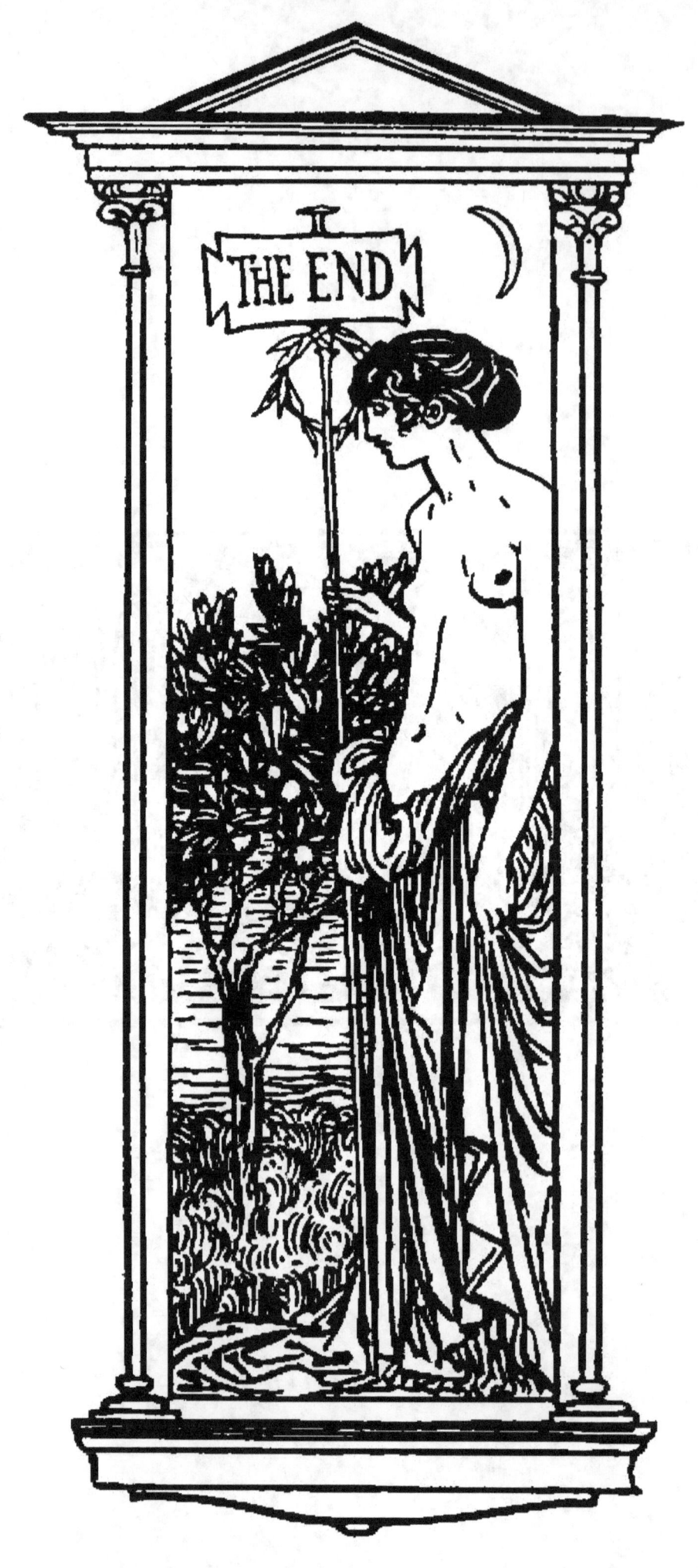

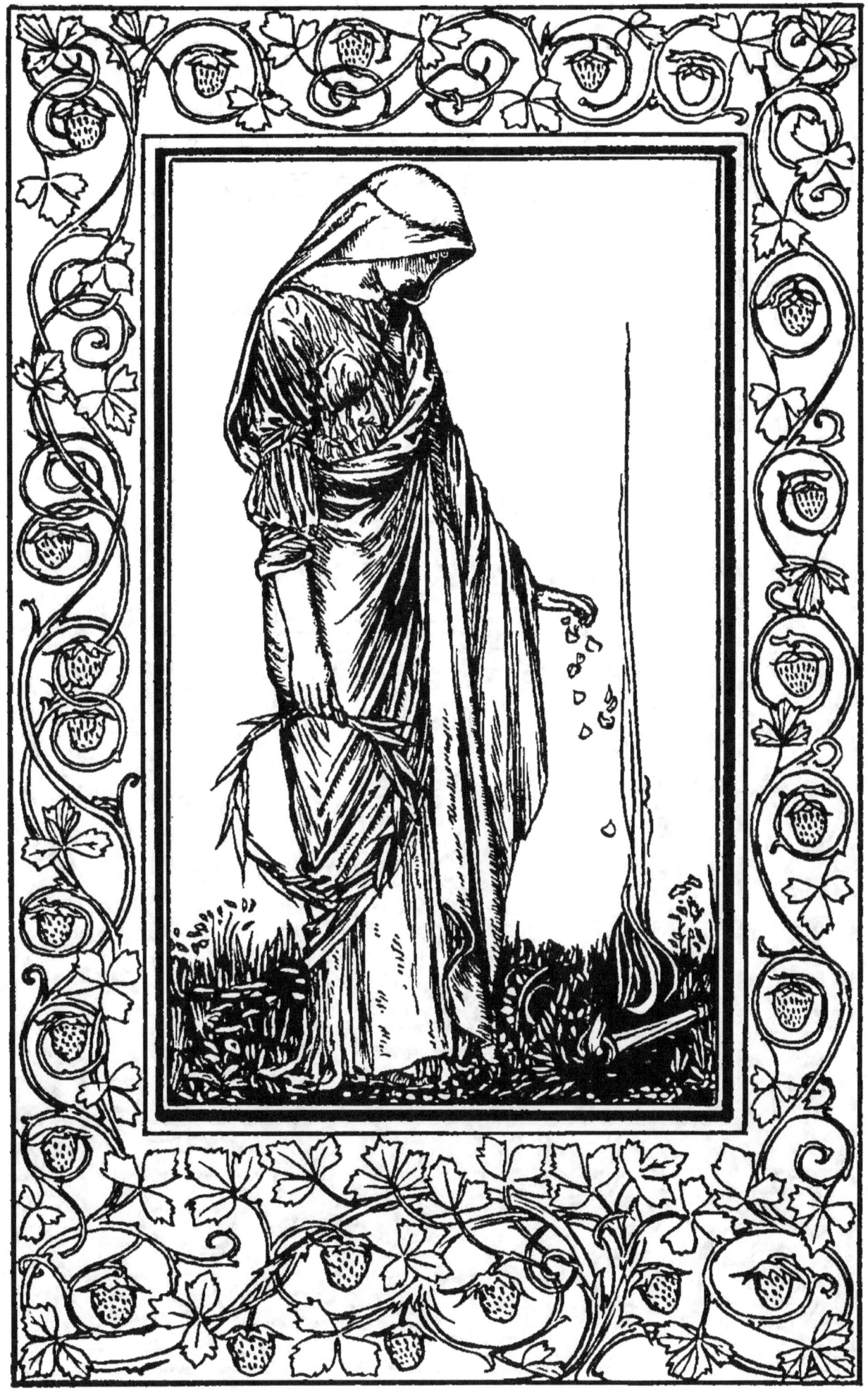

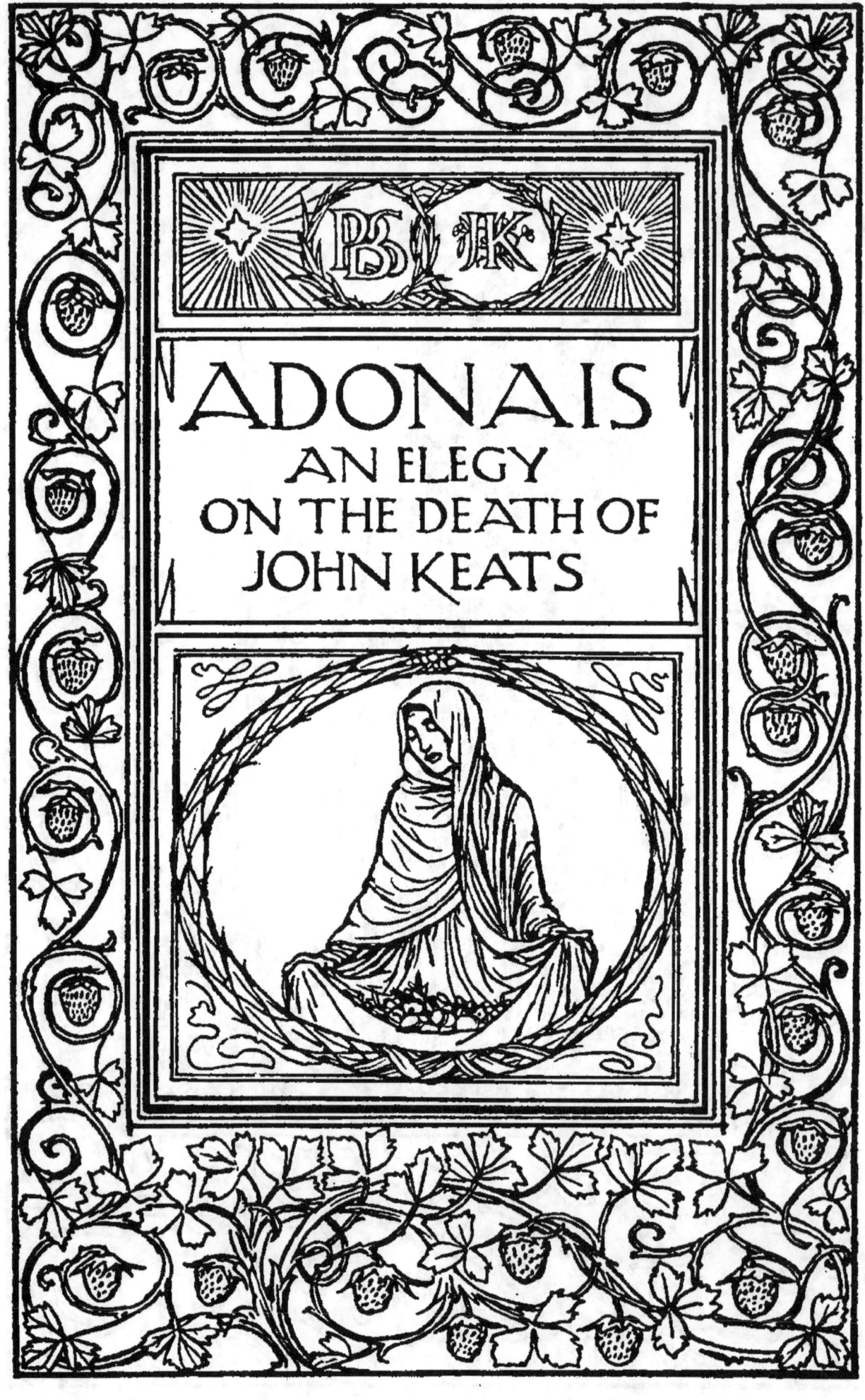

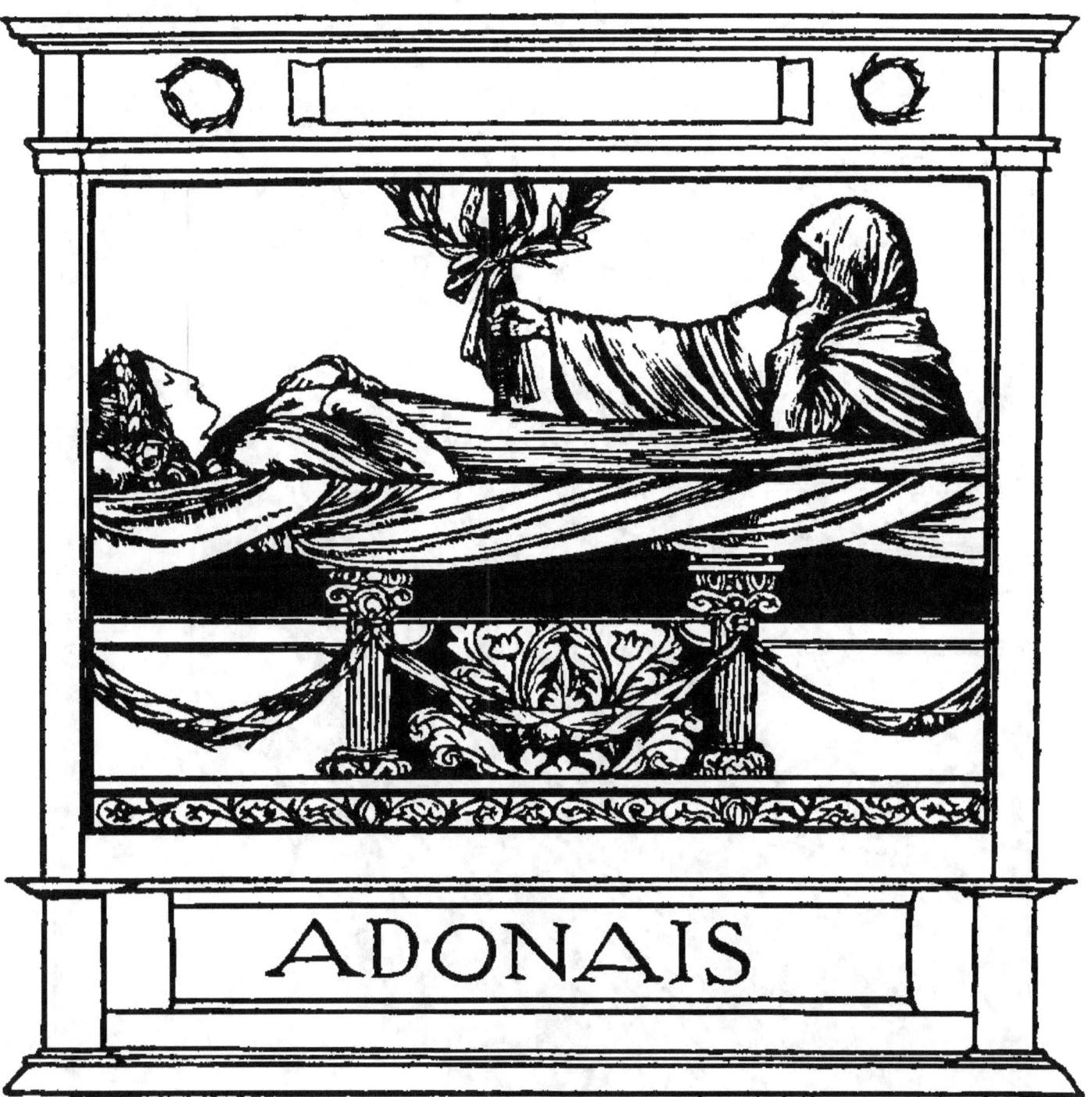

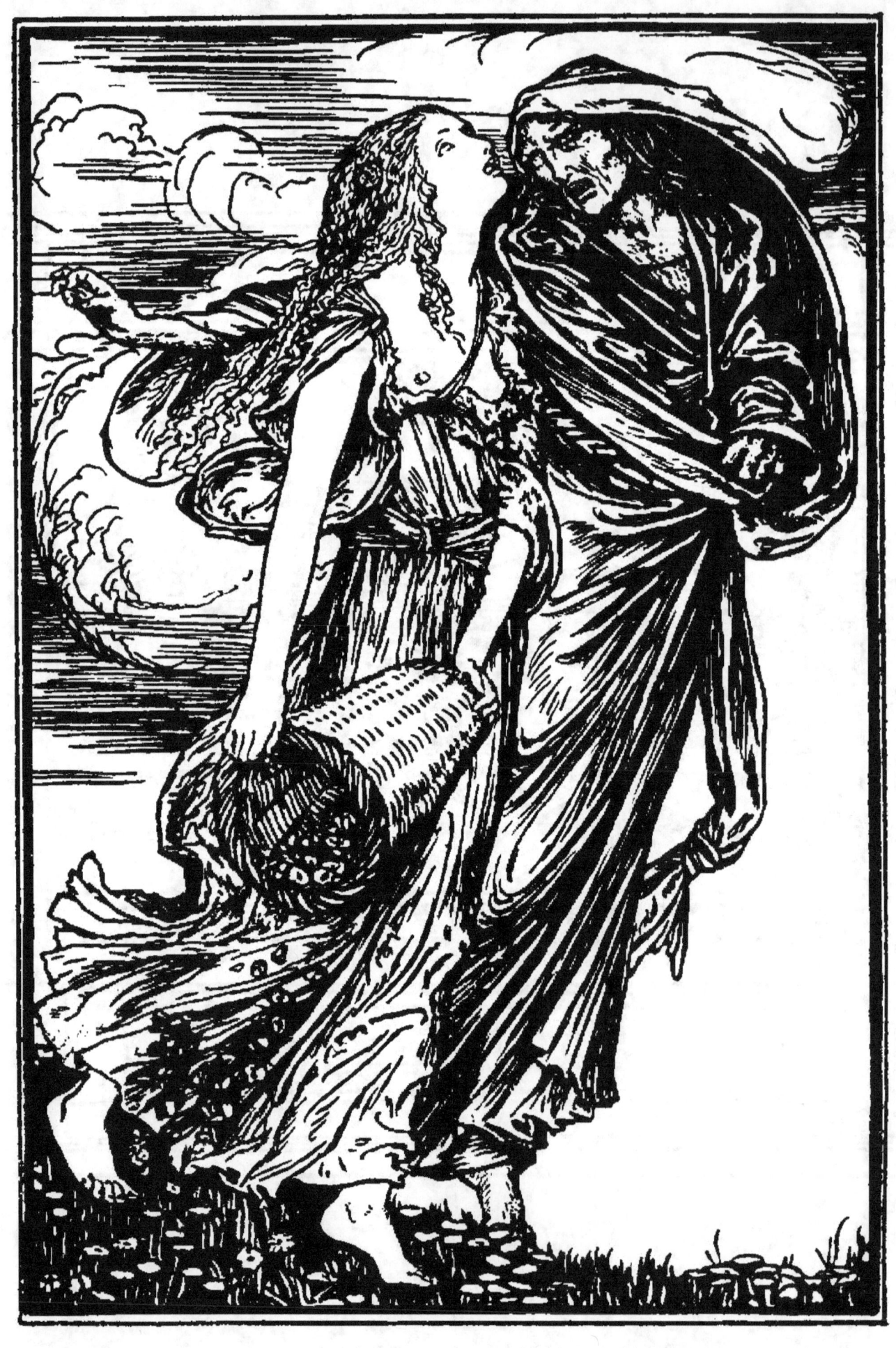

GRIEF MADE THE YOUNG SPRING WILD

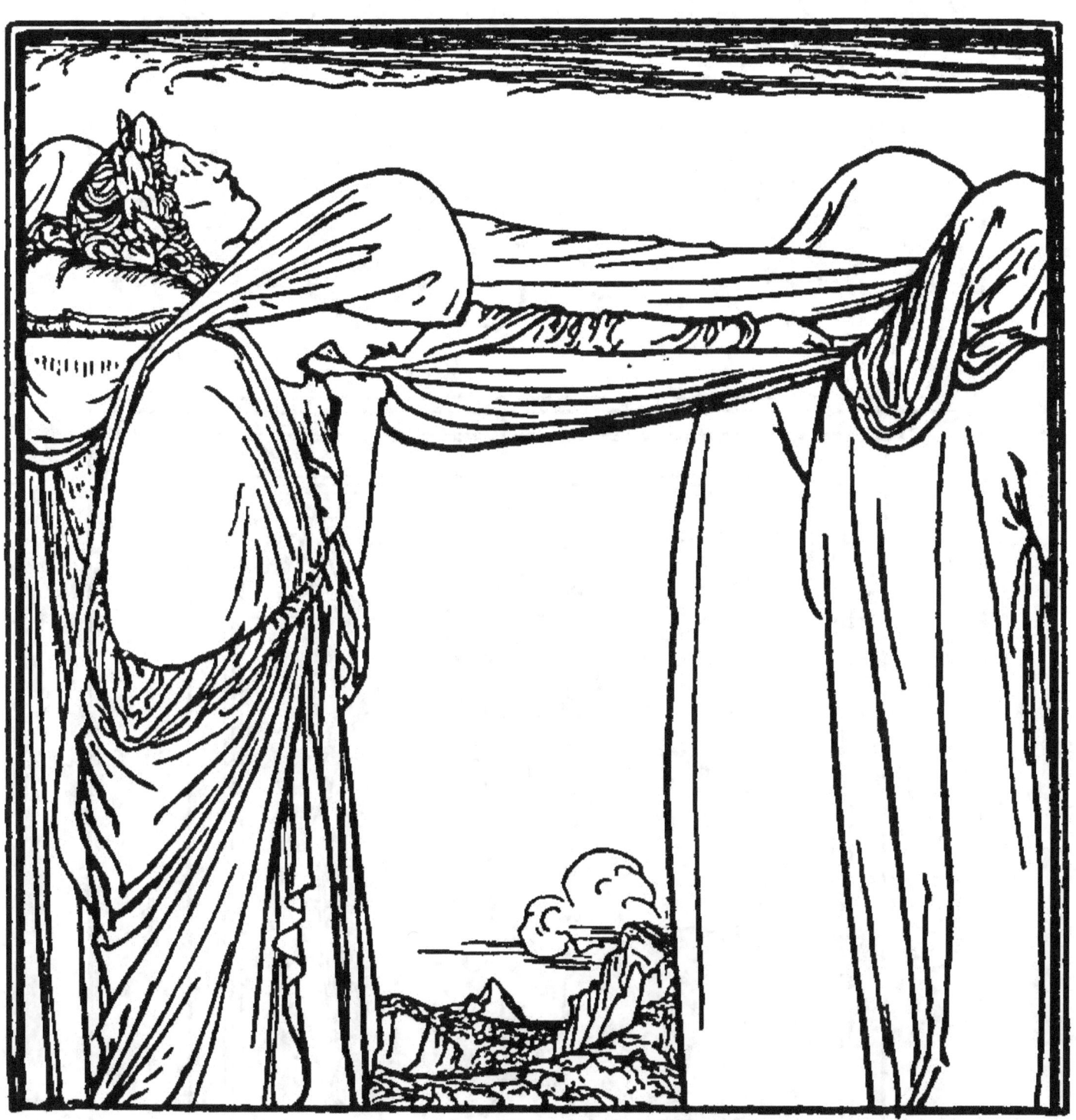

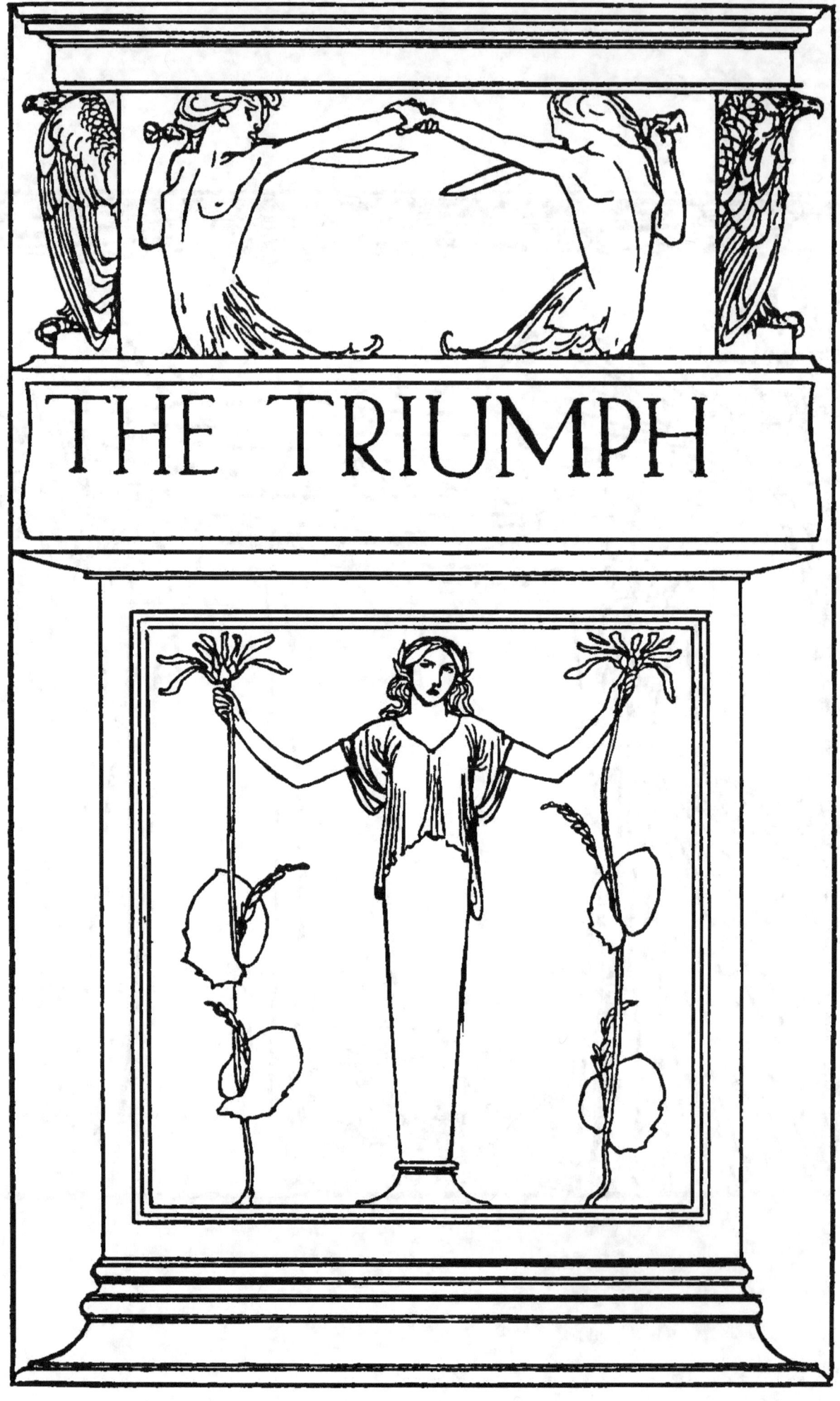

THE TRIUMPH

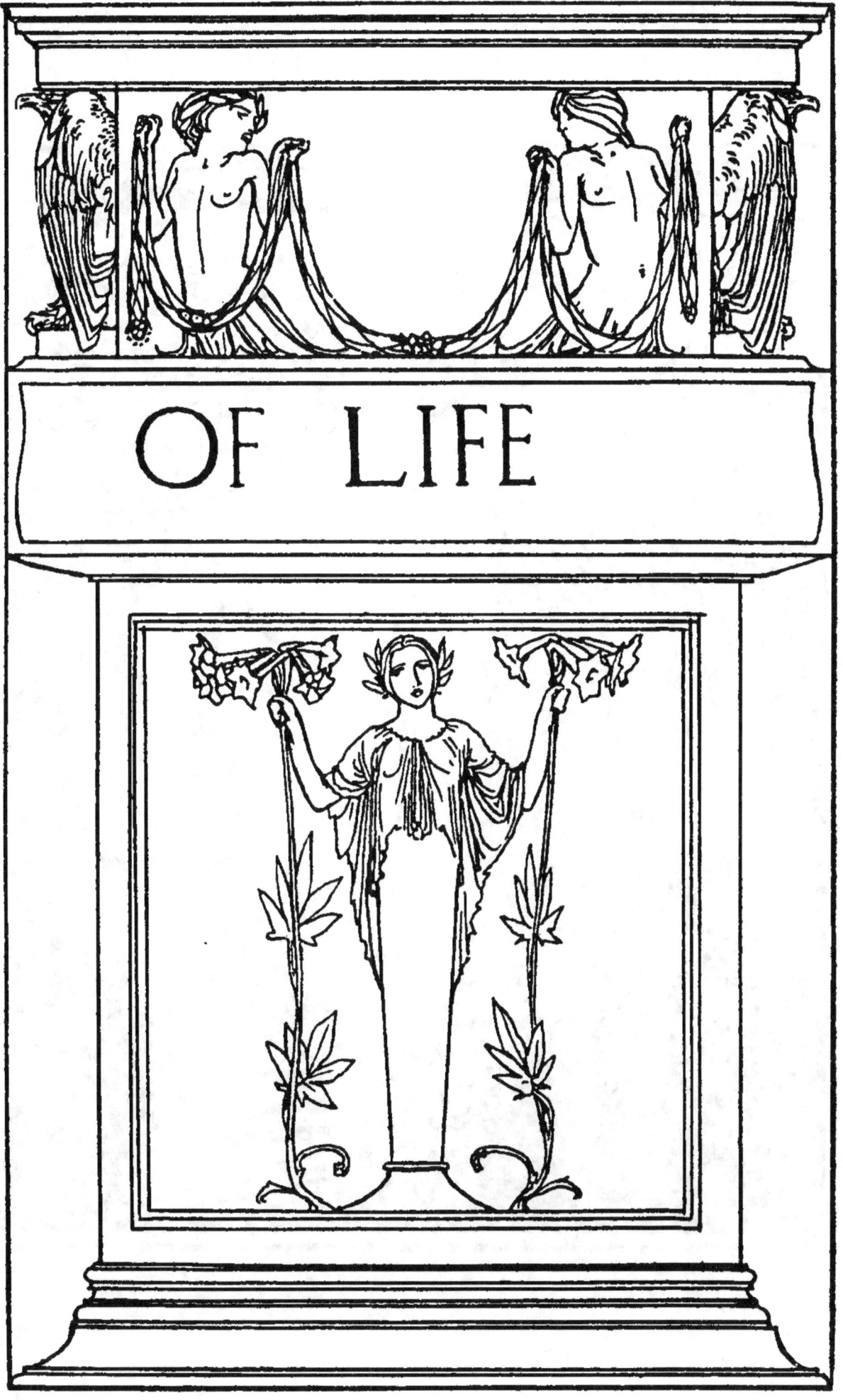

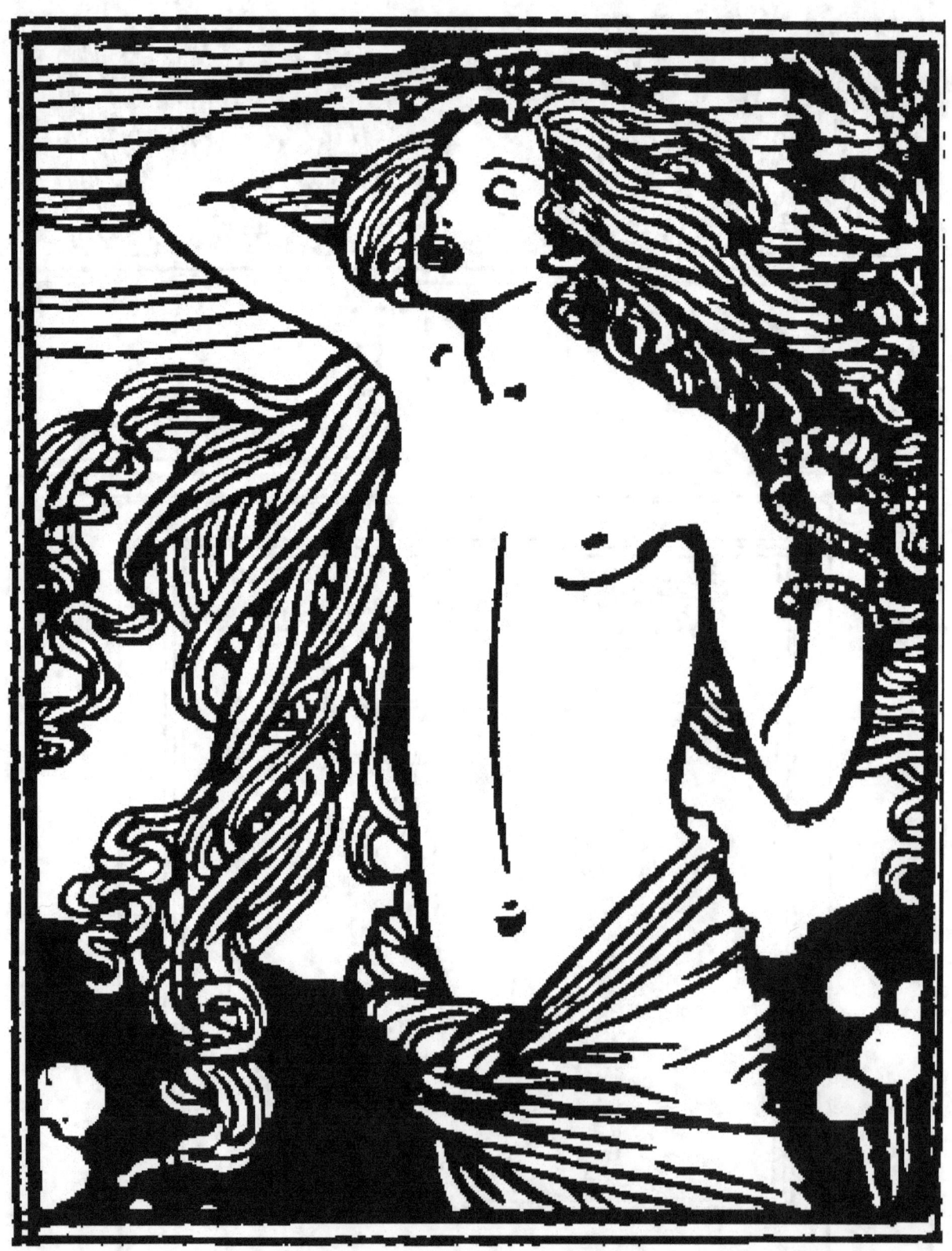

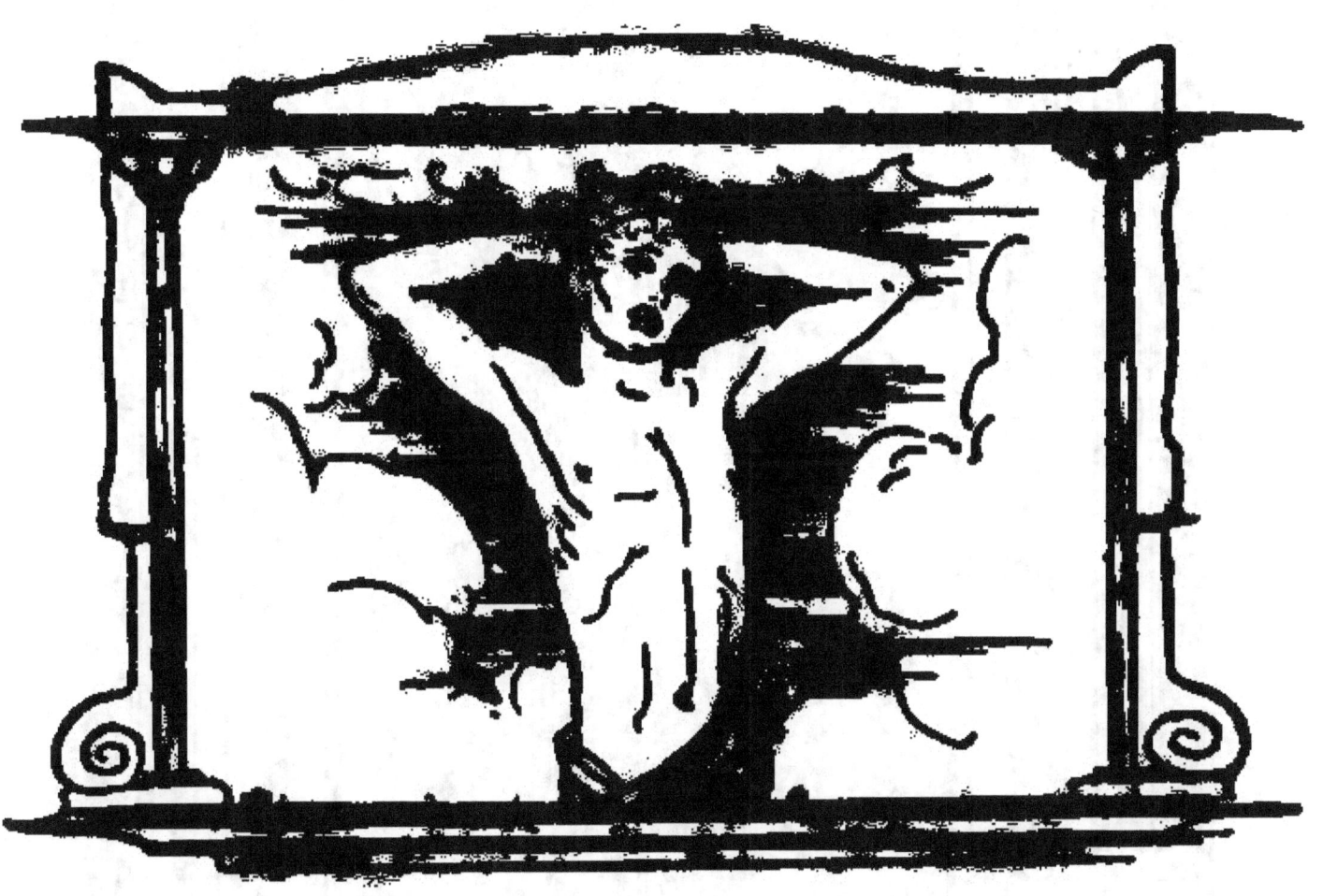

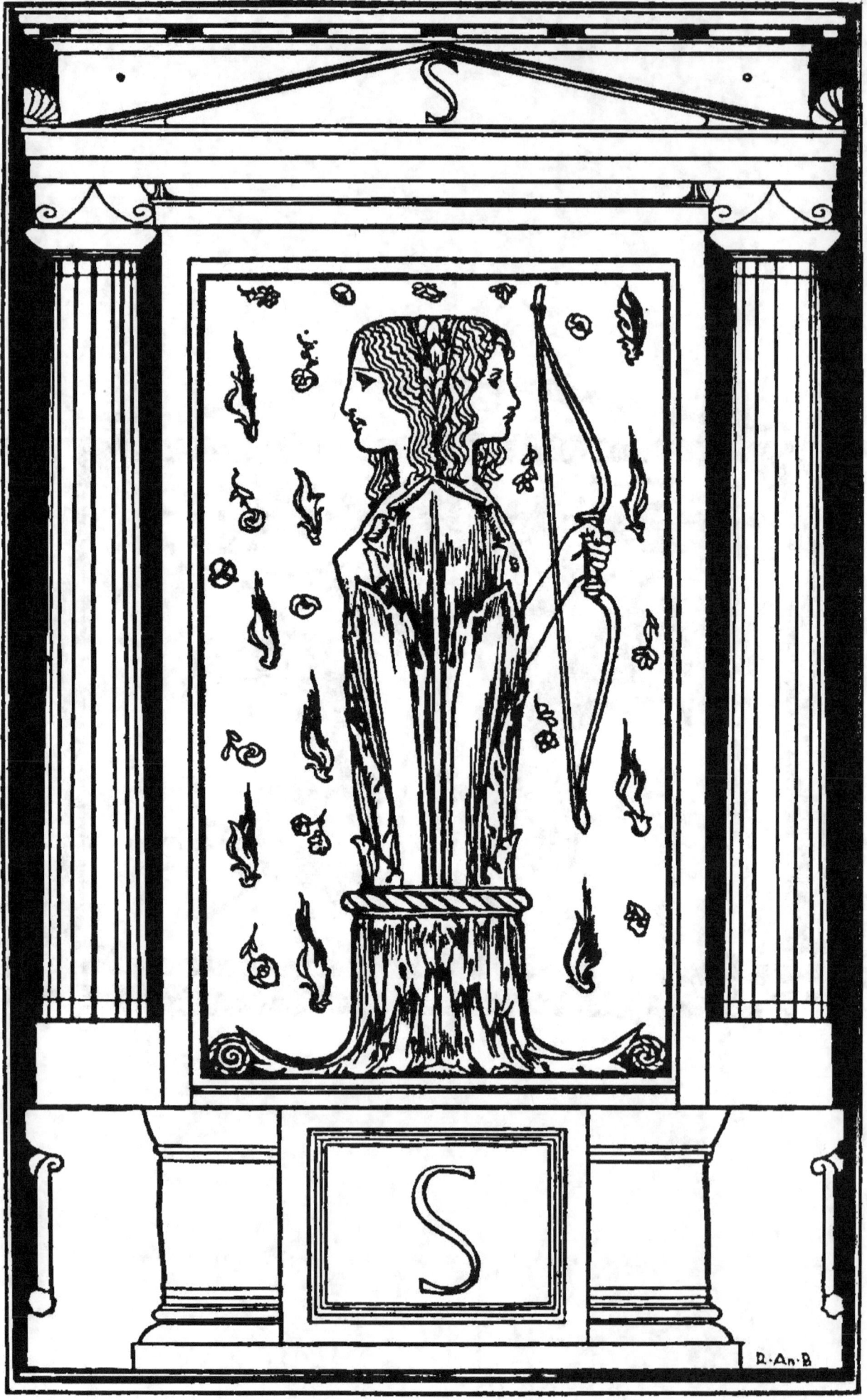

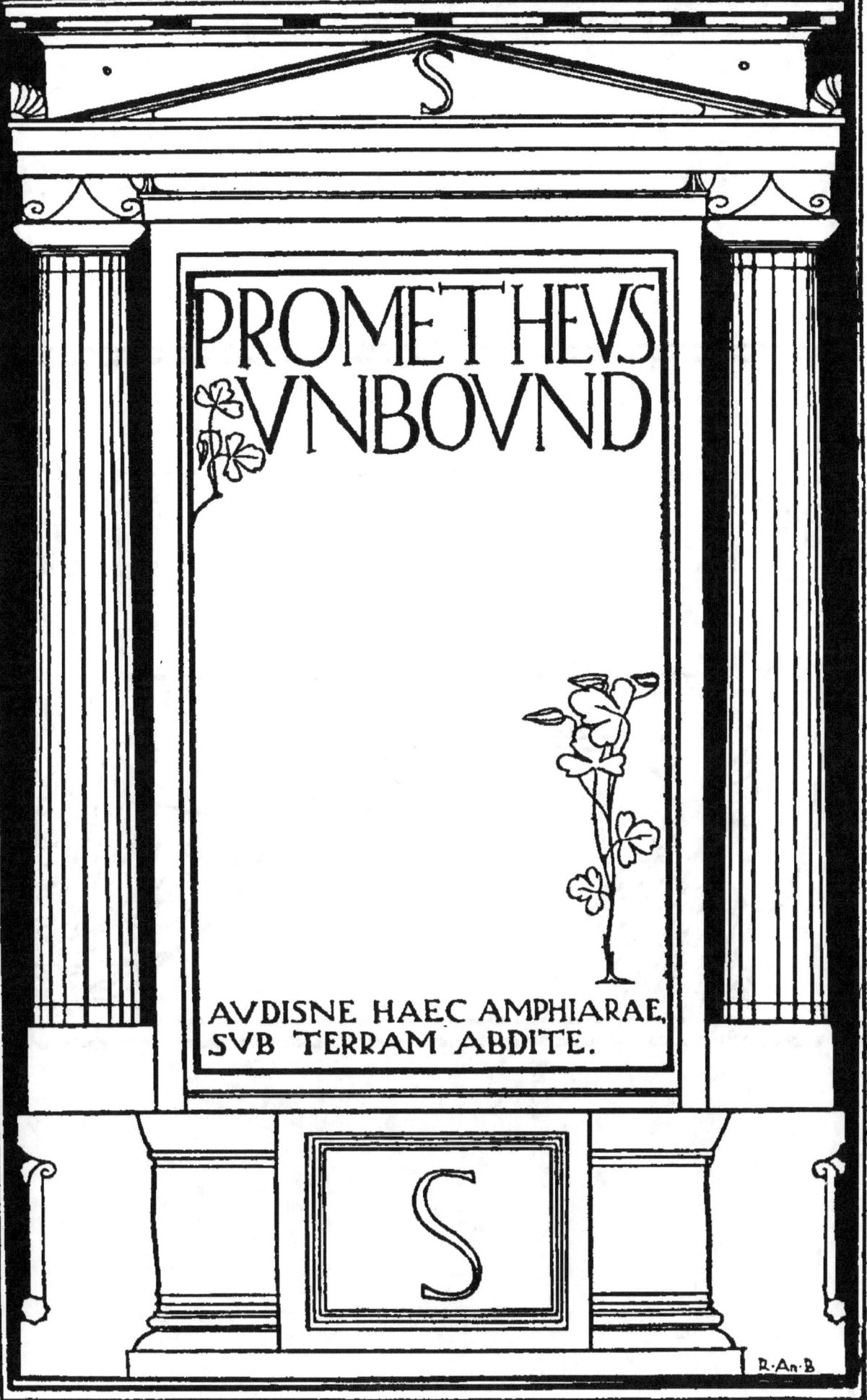

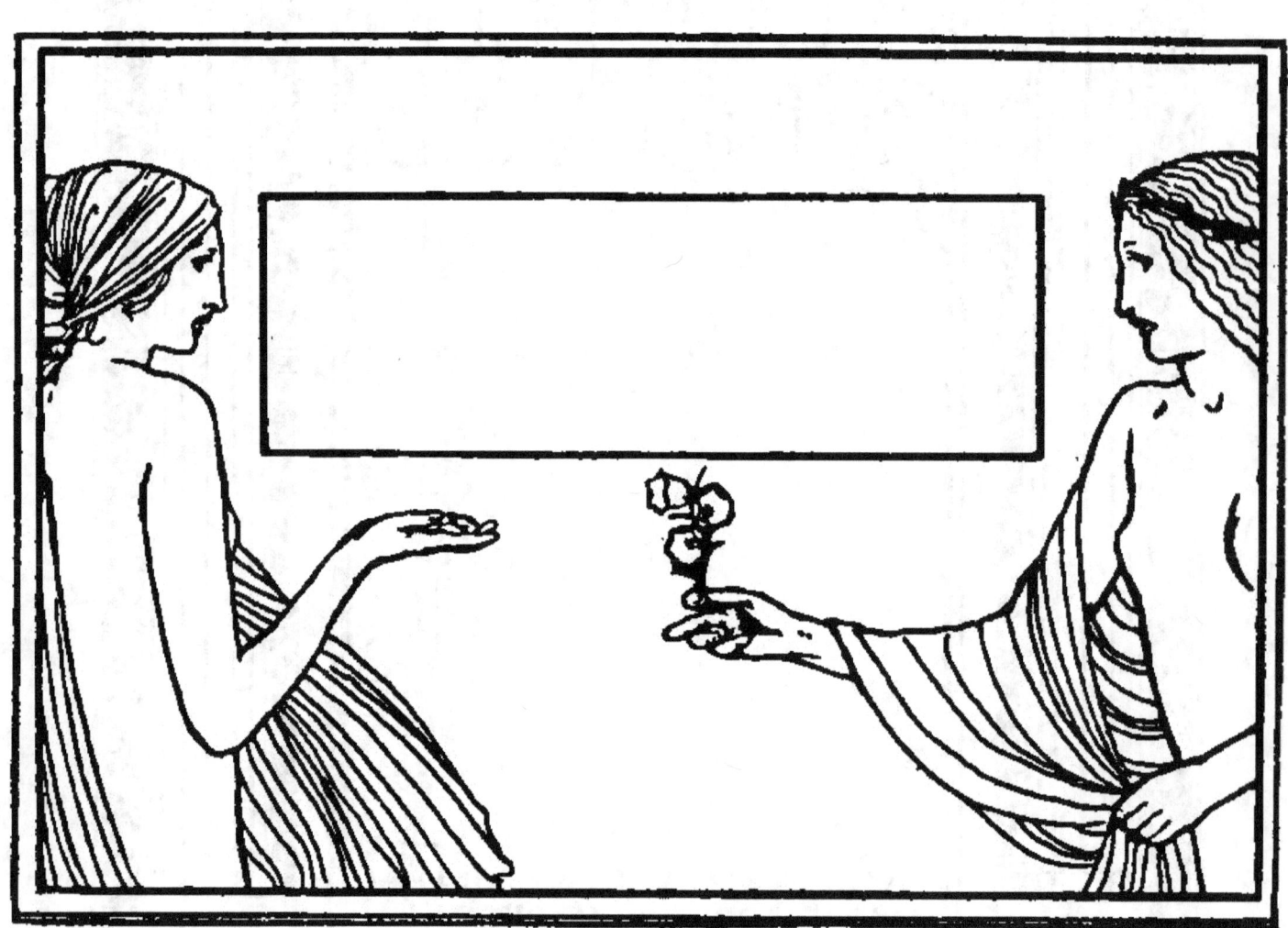

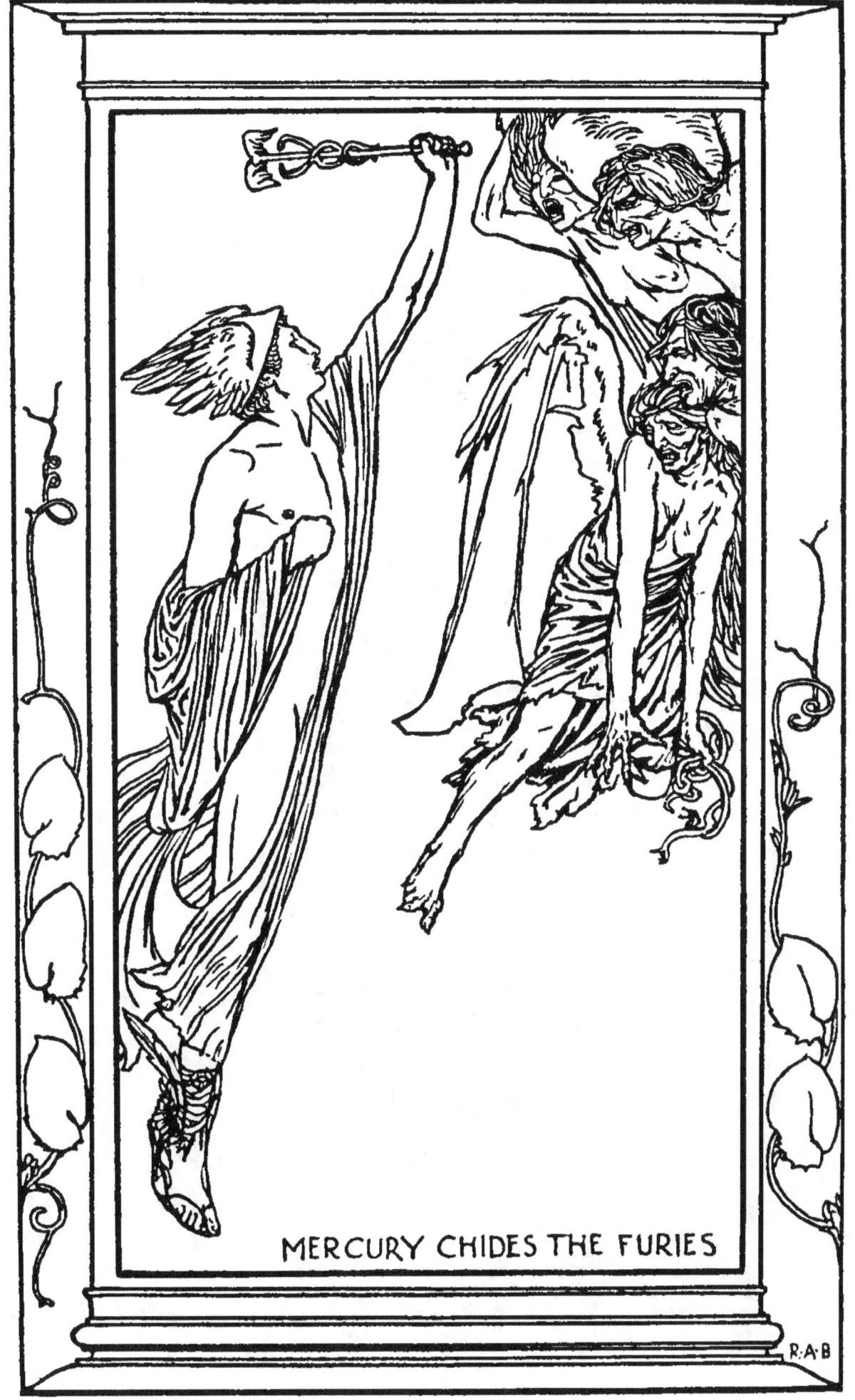

MERCURY CHIDES THE FURIES

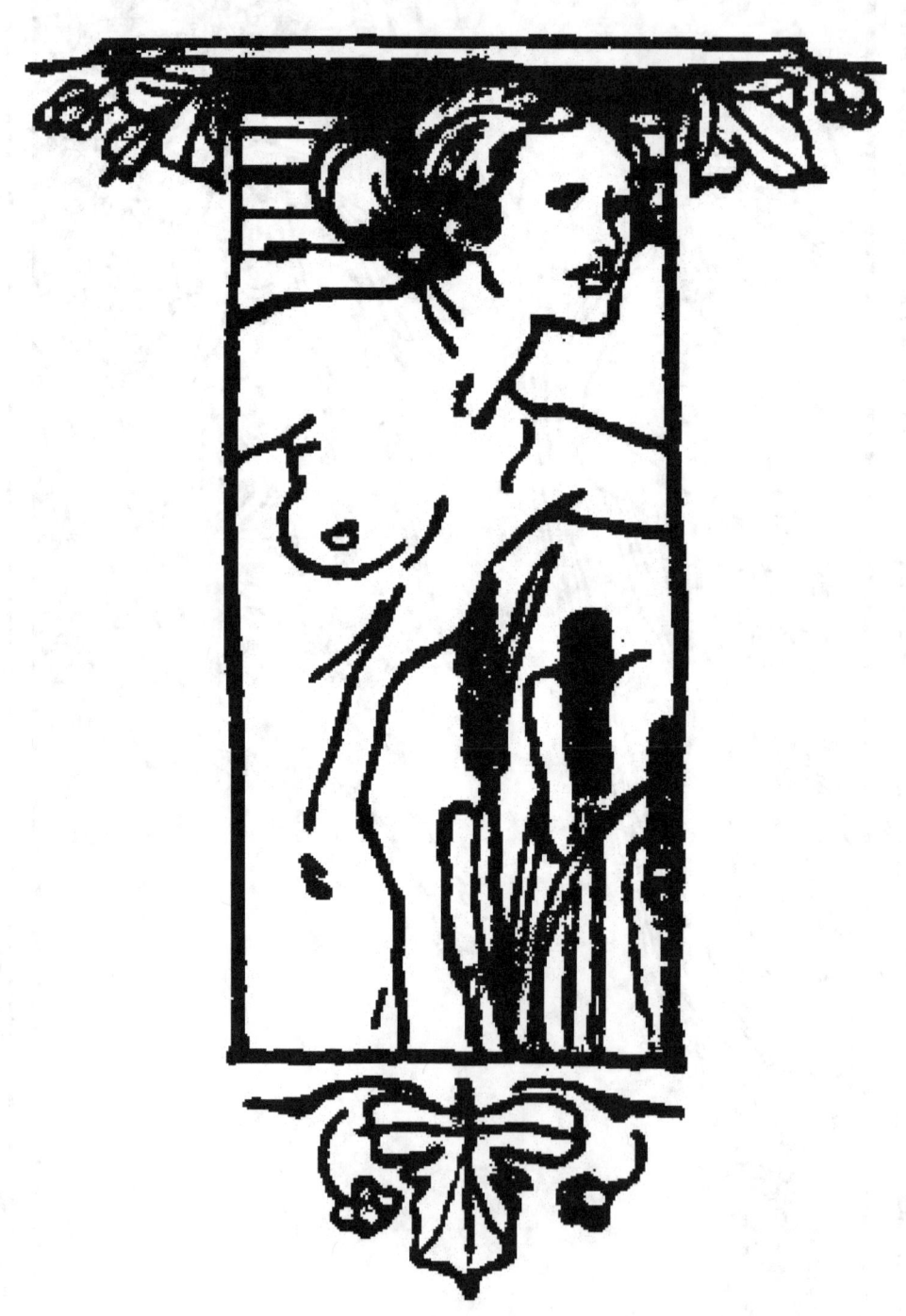

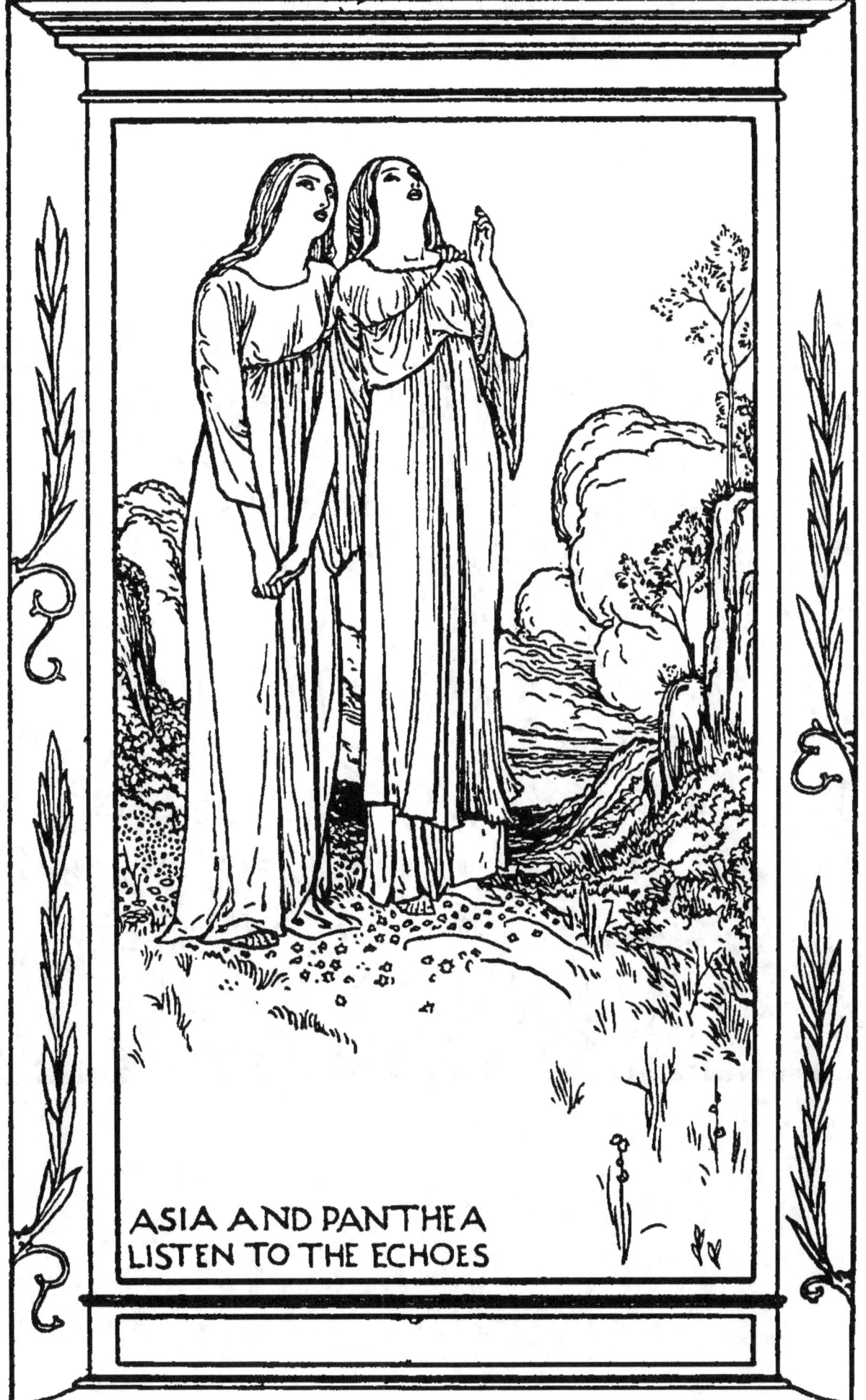

ASIA AND PANTHEA LISTEN TO THE ECHOES

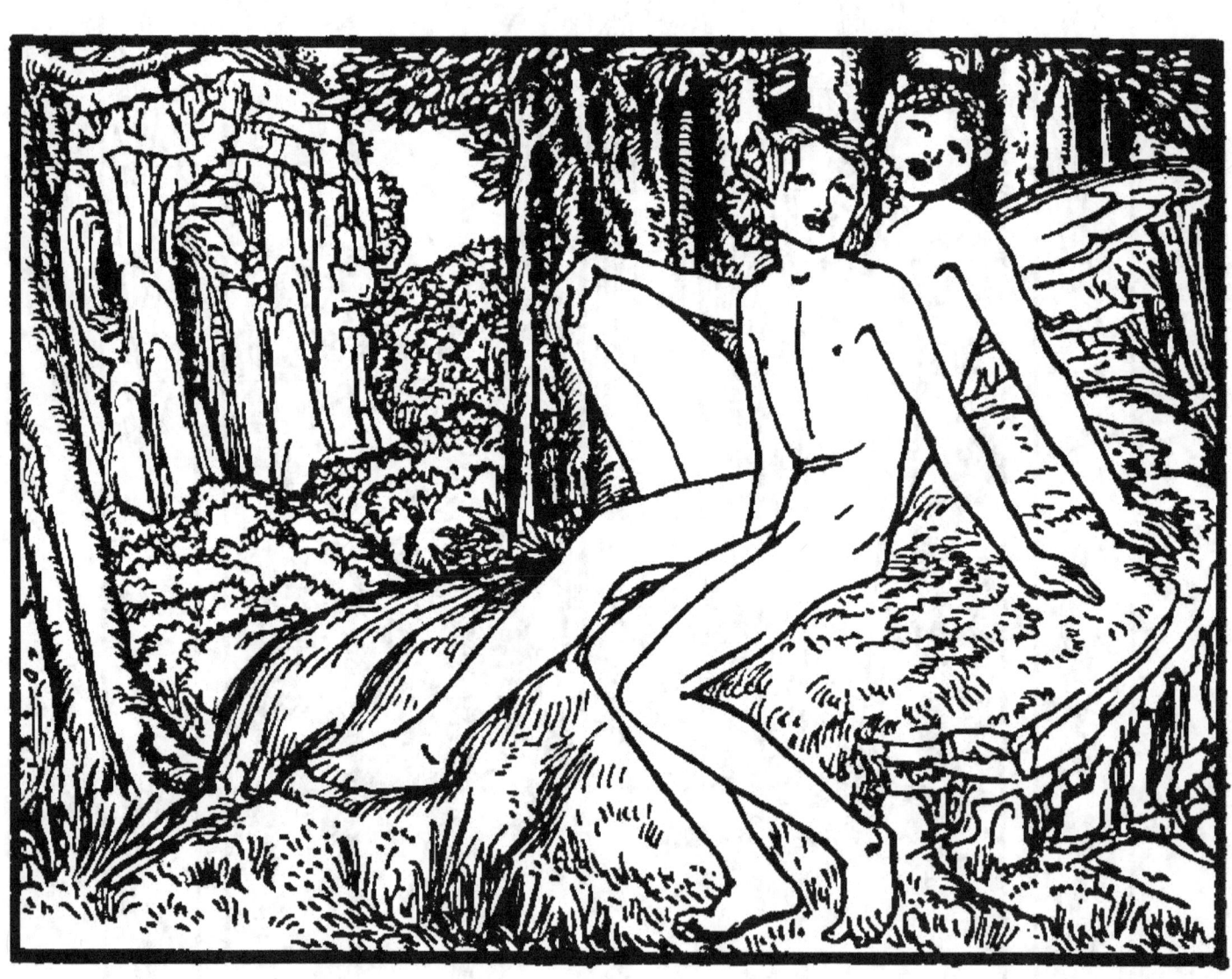

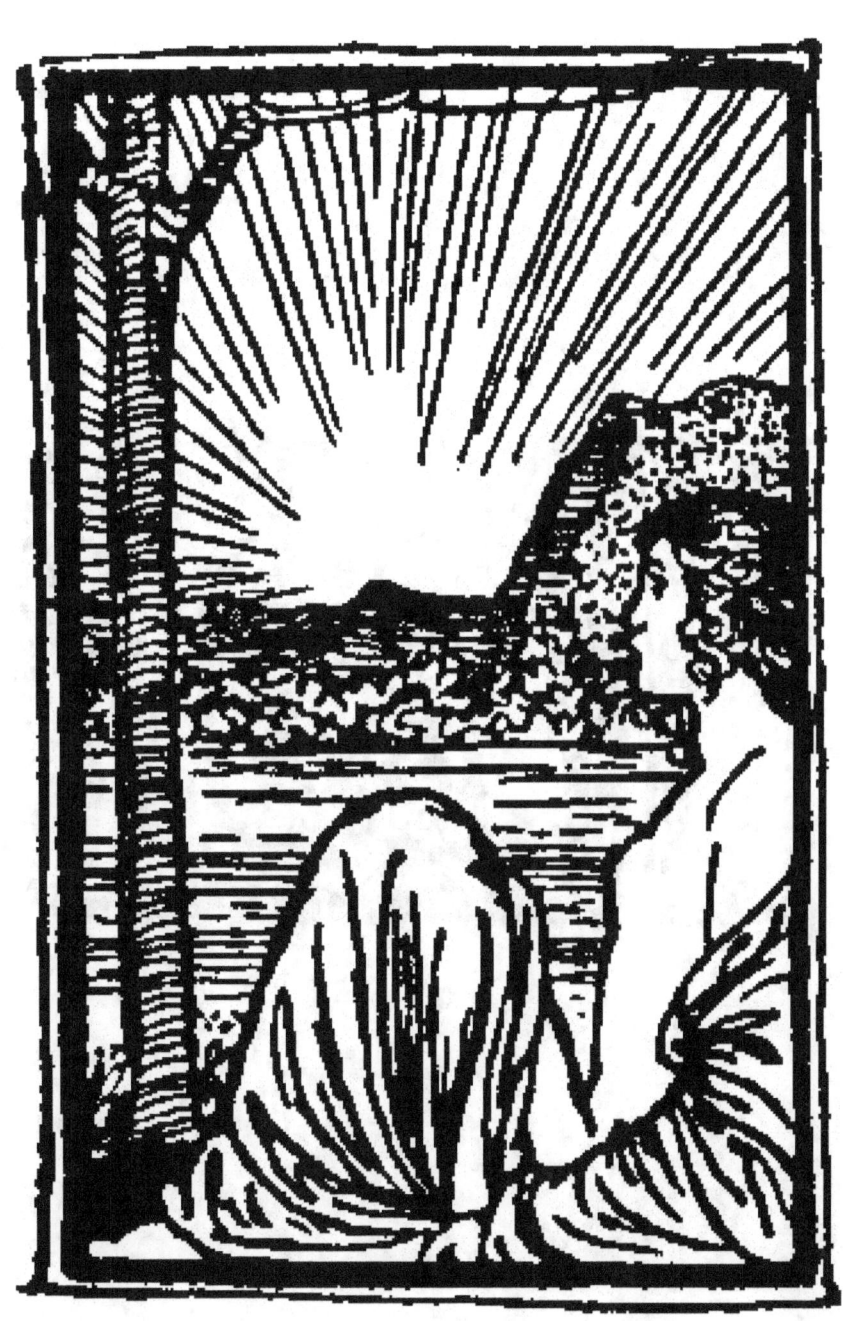

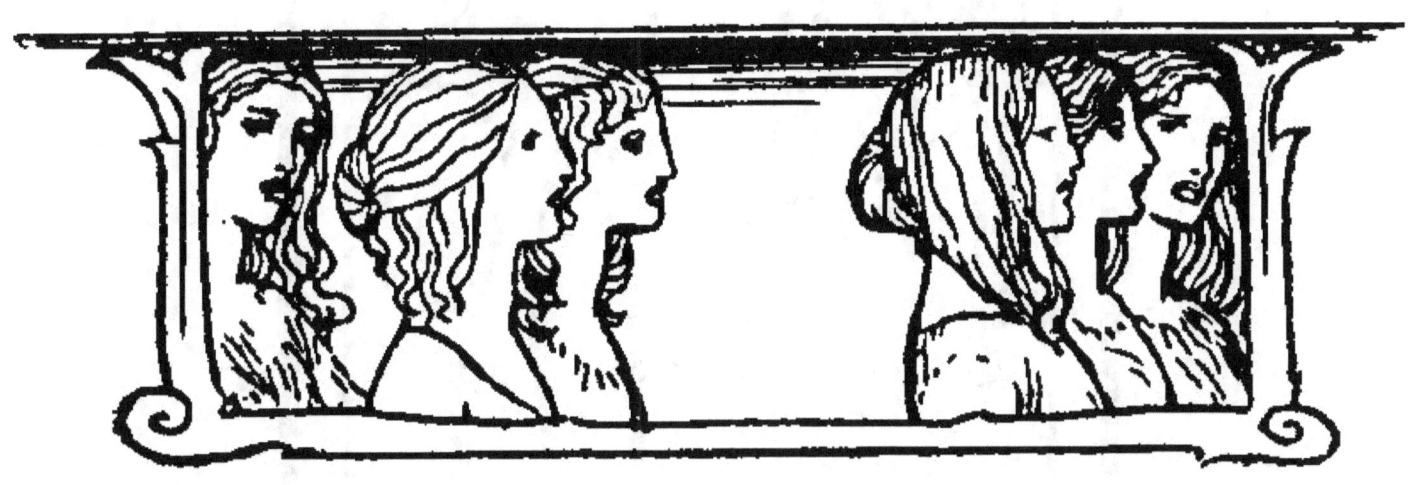

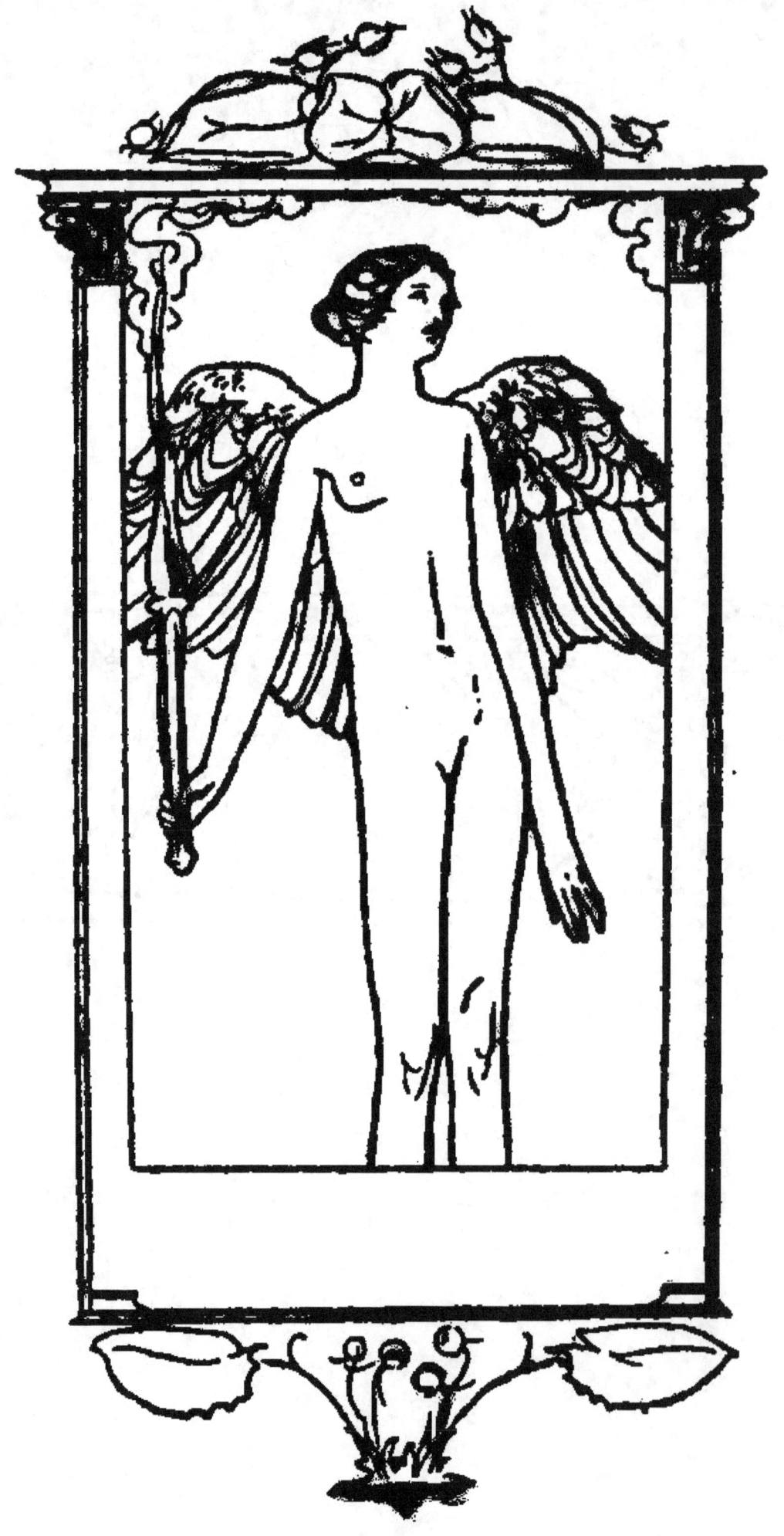

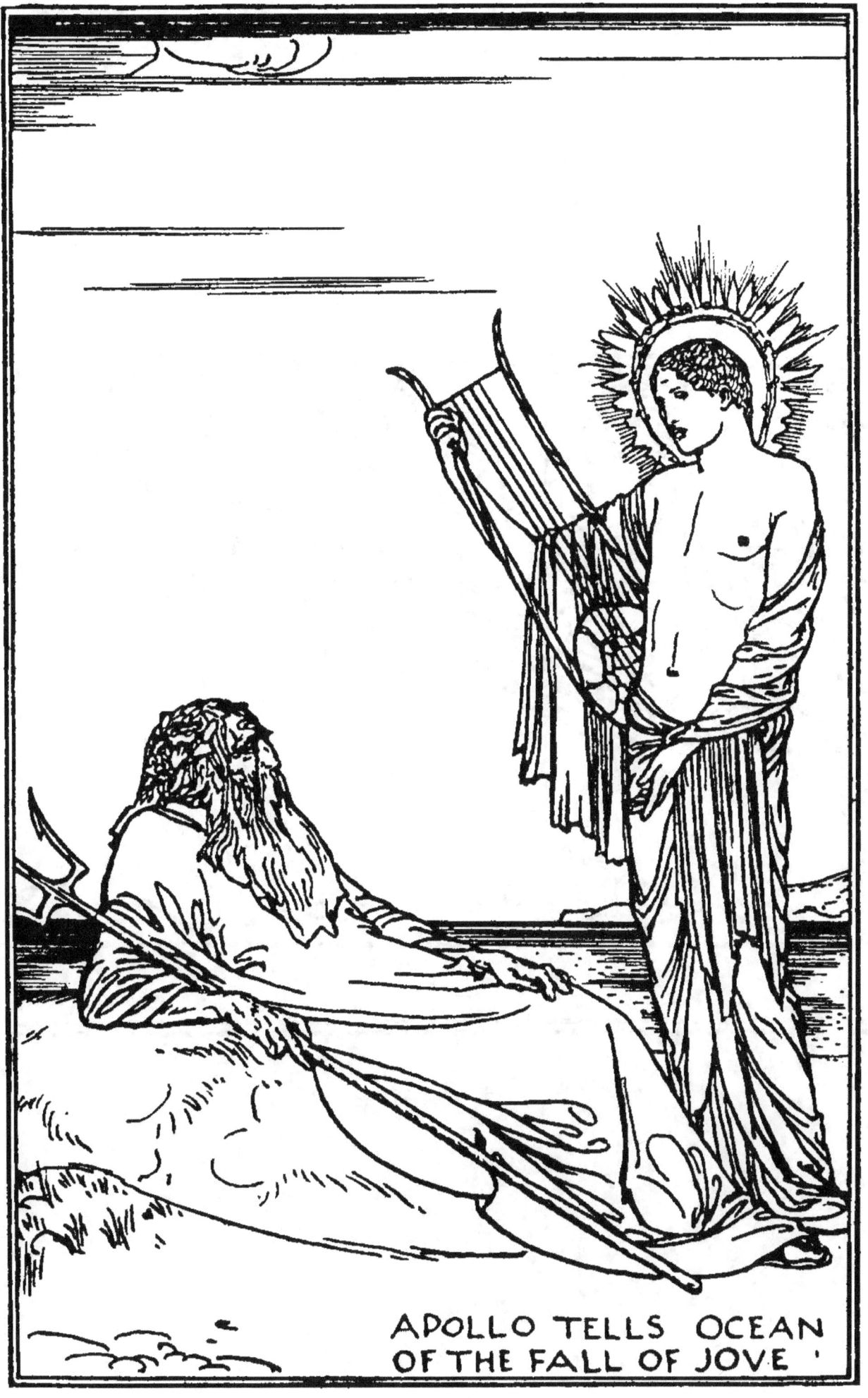

APOLLO TELLS OCEAN OF THE FALL OF JOVE

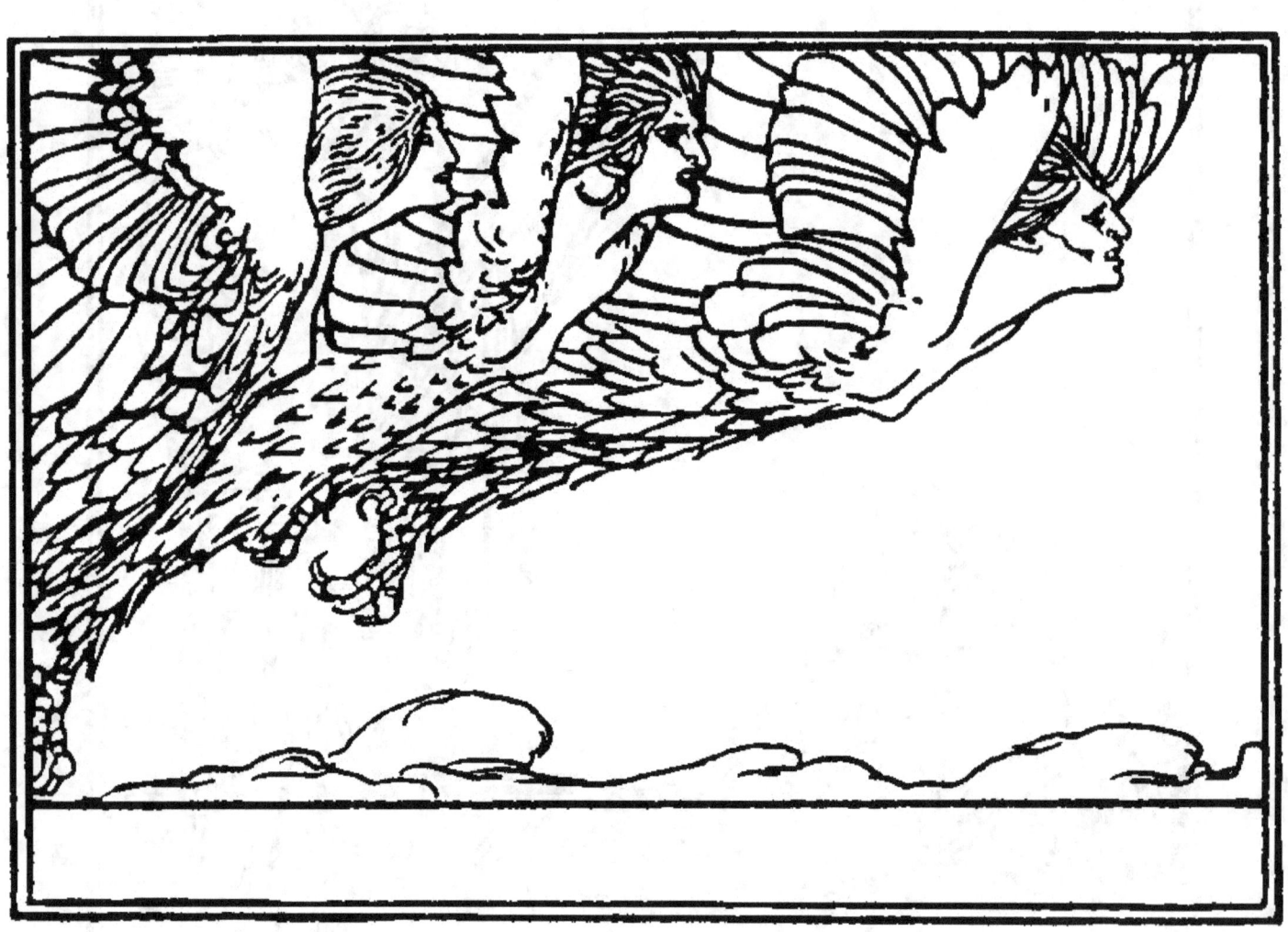

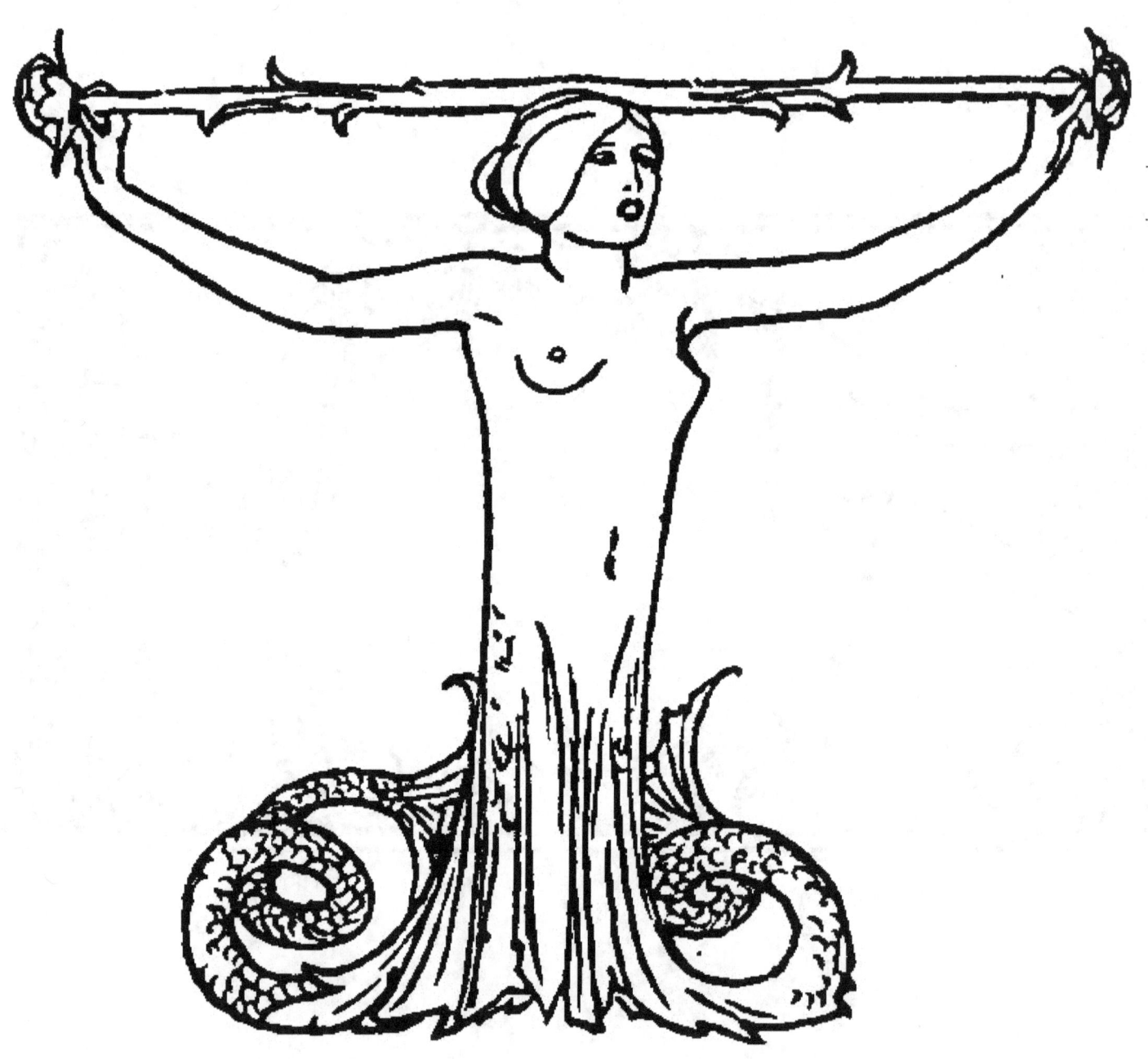

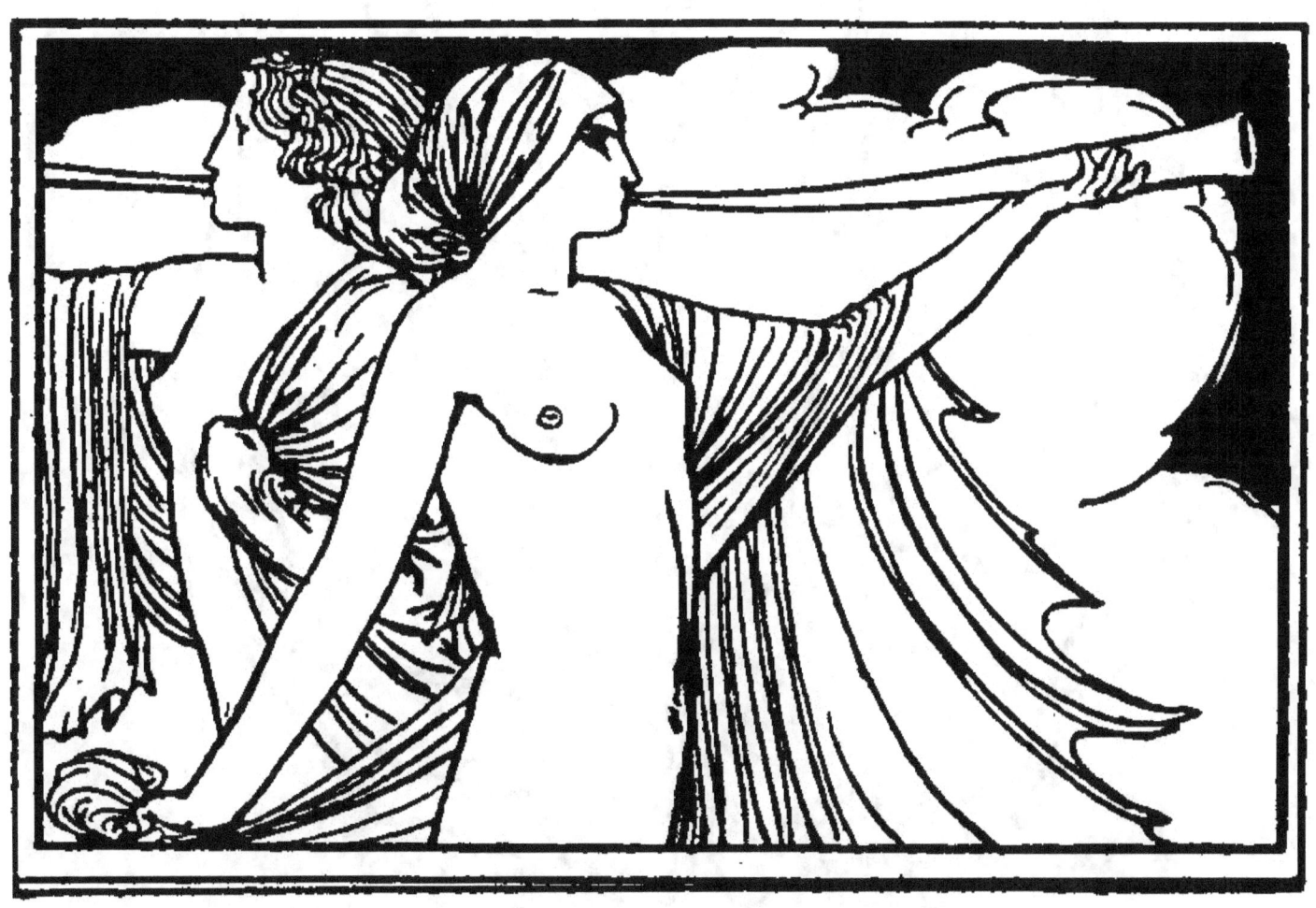

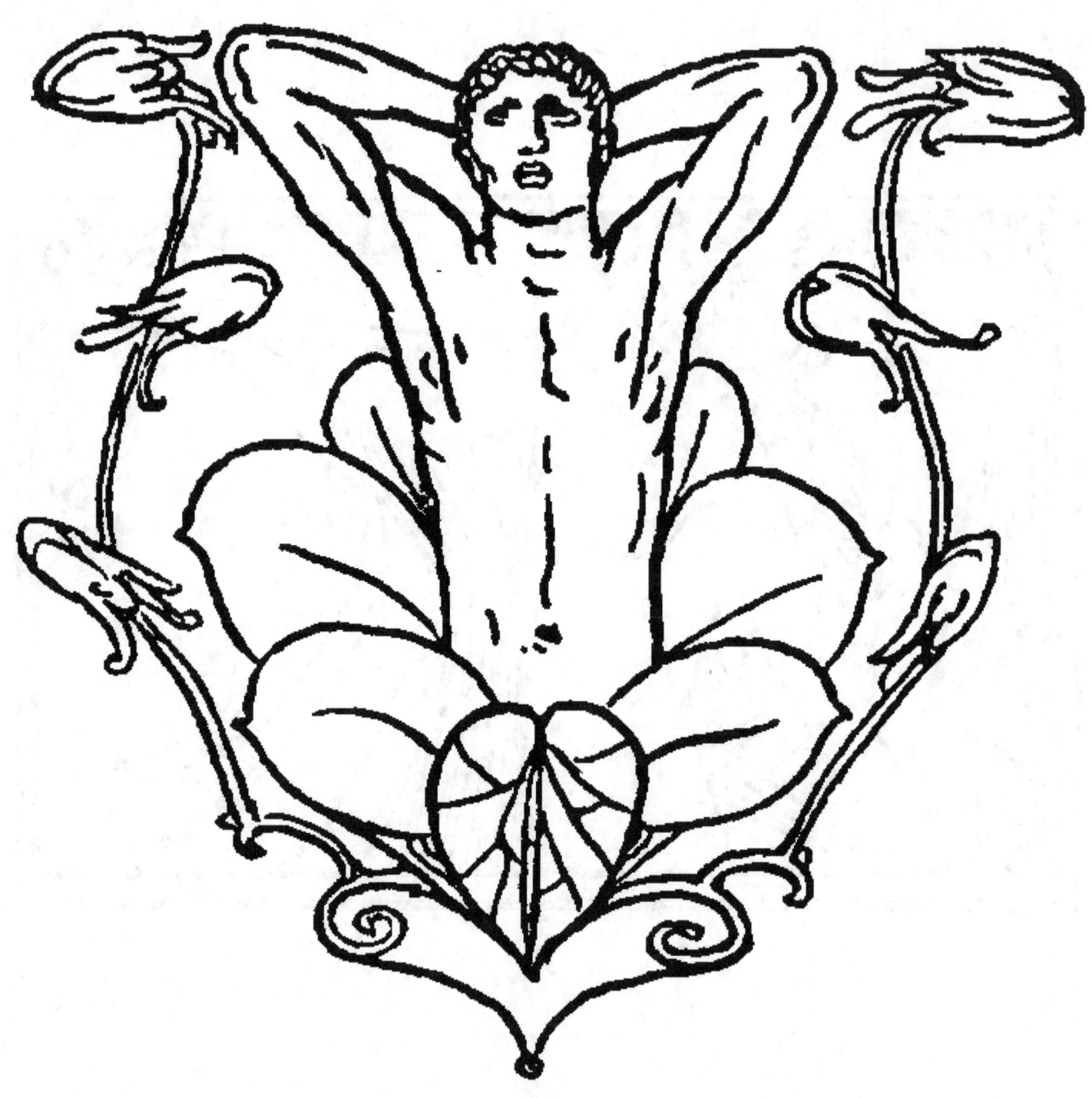

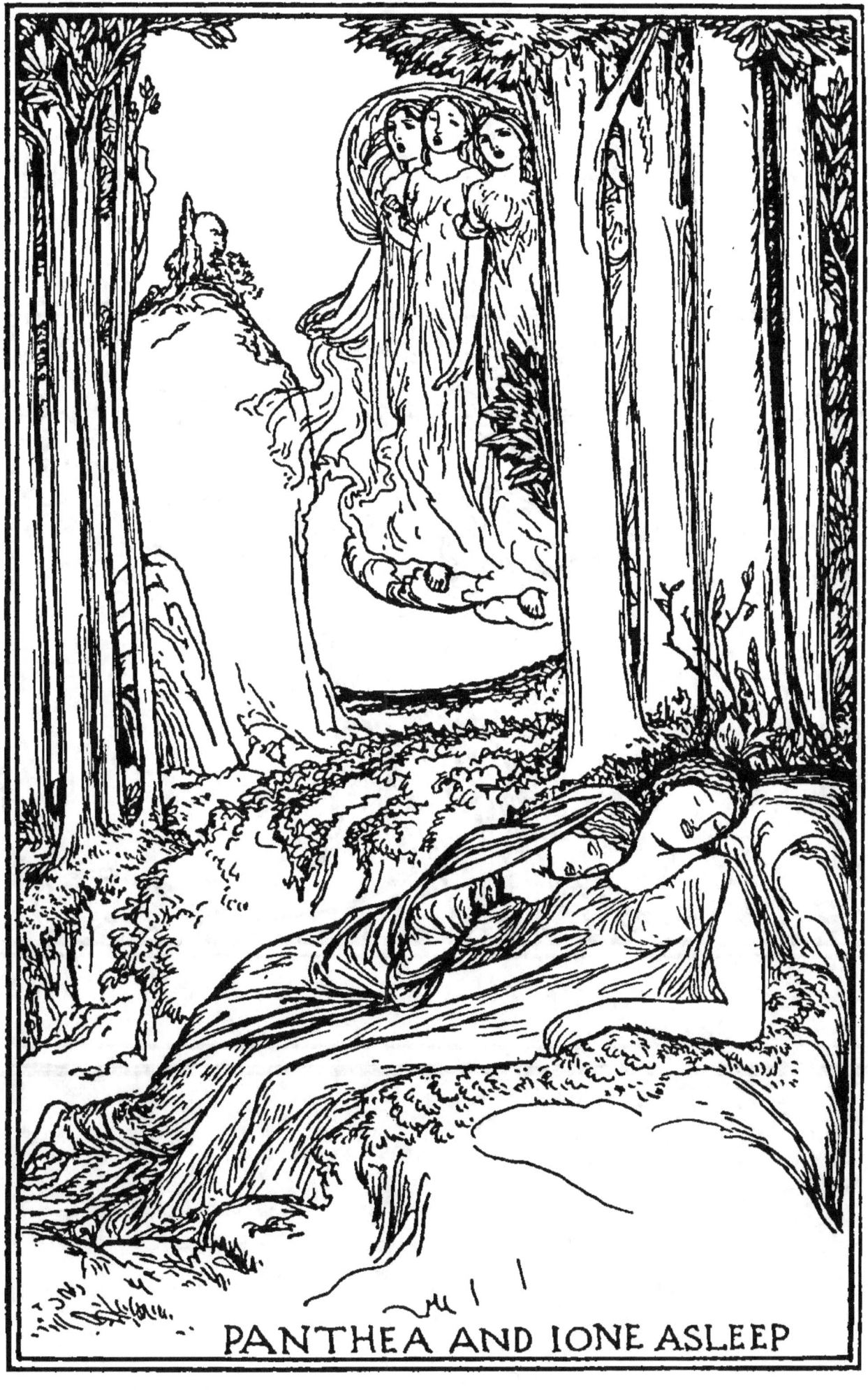

PANTHEA AND IONE ASLEEP

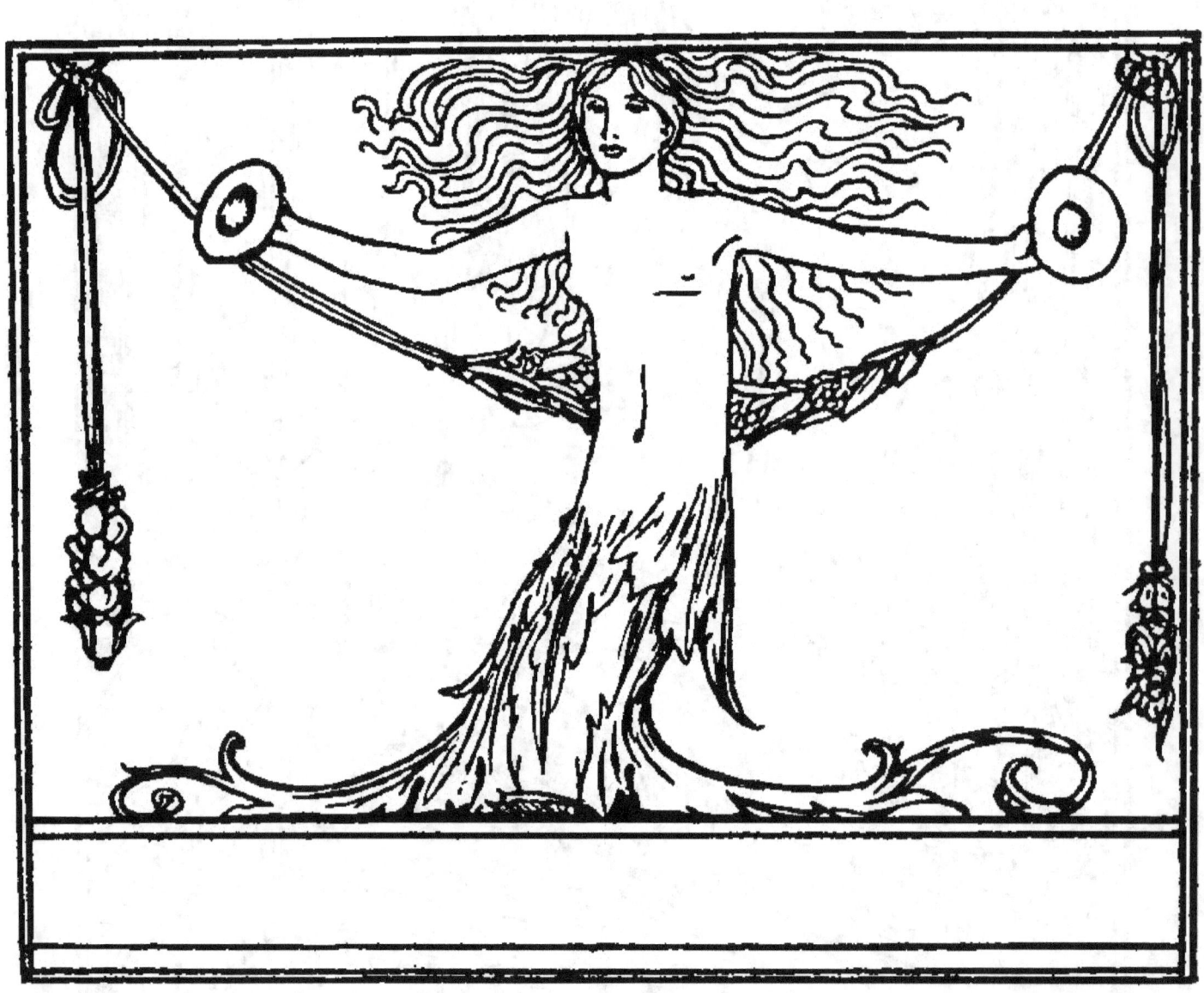

www.ingramcontent.com/pod-product-compliance
Lightning Source LLC
Chambersburg PA
CBHW082115220526
45472CB00009B/2186